Freedom?

Síreacht: Longings for Another Ireland is a series of short, topical and provocative texts on controversial issues in contemporary Ireland.

Contributors to the *Síreacht* series come from diverse backgrounds and perspectives but share a commitment to the exposition of what may often be disparaged as utopian ideas, minority perspectives on society, polity and environment, or critiques of received wisdom. Associated with the phrase *ceól sírechtach síde* found in Irish medieval poetry, *síreacht* refers to yearnings such as those evoked by the music of the *aos sí*, the supernatural people of Irish mythology. As the title for this series, we use it to signify longings for and imaginings of a better world in the spirit of the World Social Forums that 'another world is possible'. At the heart of the mythology of the *sí* is the belief that laying beneath this world is the other world. So too these texts address the urgent challenge to imagine potential new societies and relationships, but also to recognise the seeds of these other worlds in what already exists.

Other published titles in the series are

Public Sphere by Harry Browne
Commemoration by Heather Laird

The editors of the series, Órla O'Donovan, Fiona Dukelow and Rosie Meade, School of Applied Social Studies, University College Cork, welcome suggestions or proposals for consideration as future titles in the series. Please see http://sireacht.ie/ for more information.

Freedom?

by TWO FUSE

Series Editors:
Órla O'Donovan, Fiona Dukelow and Rosie Meade

CORK UNIVERSITY PRESS

First published in 2018 by
Cork University Press
Youngline Industrial Estate
Pouladuff Road, Togher
Cork T12 HT6V, Ireland

British Library Cataloguing in Publication Data
A CIP catalogue record for this book is available from the British
Library.

ISBN- 9781782052395

Typeset by Studio 10 Design
Printed by Hussar Books in Poland

CONTENTS

FIGURES

Figure 1: *Anonymous; Reading, Narrative & Memory,* by What's the Story? Collective, Rialto, 2008. Video stills by Enda O'Brien. Collaged by Fiona Whelan. © Fiona Whelan and Rialto Youth Project.

Figure 2: *The Day in Question*, by What's the Story? Collective, Irish Museum of Modern Art, Dublin, 2009. Video still by Enda O'Brien. © Fiona Whelan and Rialto Youth Project.

Figure 3: *Policing Dialogues*, by What's the Story? Collective, The LAB, Dublin, 2010. Photograph by Michael Durand. © Dublin City Council Arts Office.

Figure 4: *Policing Dialogues*, by What's the Story? Collective, The LAB, Dublin, 2010. © Fiona Whelan.

Figure 5: *Natural History of Hope*, by Fiona Whelan, Rialto Youth Project and Brokentalkers, Project Arts Centre, Dublin, 2016. © Ray Hegarty.

Figure 6: *The Day in Question,* by What's the Story? Collective, Irish Museum of Modern Art, Dublin, 2009. Video still by Enda O'Brien. © Fiona Whelan and Rialto Youth Project.

Figure 7: *Policing Dialogues*, by What's the Story? Collective, The LAB, Dublin, 2010. Photograph by Michael Durand. © Dublin City Council Arts Office.

Figure 8: *Natural History of Hope*, by Fiona Whelan, Rialto Youth Project and Brokentalkers, Project Arts Centre, Dublin, 2016. © Ray Hegarty.

Figure 9: *Natural History of Hope*, by Fiona Whelan, Rialto Youth Project and Brokentalkers, Project Arts Centre, Dublin, 2016. Programme design by Unthink. © Chris Maguire.

Figure 10: *Natural History of Hope*, by Fiona Whelan, Rialto Youth Project and Brokentalkers, Project Arts Centre, Dublin, 2016. Video still by Paddy Cahill. © Shoot to Kill

Illustrations throughout are by Orla Whelan, 2017 (© Orla Whelan, www.whaledust.com).

ACKNOWLEDGEMENTS

At once an ethos and a method of inquiry, Two Fuse (www.twofuse.com) is a collaborative platform that brings together Kevin Ryan (who works in the discipline of sociology) and Fiona Whelan (who works in the field of socially engaged/collaborative arts) through a commitment to thinking across the boundaries of disciplinary enclosures. Two Fuse is a way of acknowledging the collaborative nature of inquiry, that the pursuit of knowledge and understanding entails both direct and indirect encounters and exchanges. We thus wish to thank the many people who have made it possible for us to engage in meaningful discussion, including the staff and management of Rialto Youth Project and partner community organisations, the residents of Rialto, An Garda Síochána, Brokentalkers theatre company, the Studio 468 team and all the individual advisors who have engaged with the practice we discuss in Section 3, including Kathleen Lynch, Martina Carroll, Niall O'Baoill, Ailbhe Murphy, Ciaran Smyth, Annette Moloney and Aogan Mulcahy.

Special acknowledgment goes to Jim Lawlor, manager of Rialto Youth Project, the members of What's the Story? Collective – Jamie Hendrick, Jonathan Myers, Gillian O'Connor, Garrett Kenny, Nichola Mooney, Graham Dunphy, Vanessa Kenny, Michael Byrne and Nicola Whelan, and the coordination group and primary cast of *Natural History of Hope* – Sharon Cooney, Nichola Mooney, Michelle Dunne, Gillian O'Connor, Dannielle McKenna,

Audrey Wade, Lydia Lynam, Niamh Tracey, Vicky White, Lisa Graham and Amy White – all of whom have been long-time collaborators of Fiona's. The practice discussed in Section 3 received funding from multiple sources over a decade, all of which are listed on fionawhelan.com. Special thanks are due to the Arts Council of Ireland for regular support.

Thanks also to Barry Devlin, Horslips, and Crashed Music for permission to use the quote from Horslips' album *Aliens* in the introduction to this book (© Horslips Records).

Section 2 is an expanded and revised version of an article by Kevin Ryan published in the *Journal of Political Power* as 'Academic Freedom and the Eye of Power' (2016), © Taylor & Francis, available online: http://www.tandfon line.com, article DOI: 10.1080/2158379X.2016.1191162.

Section 4 is a series of excerpts from *Natural History of Hope*, a live performance from Fiona Whelan, Rialto Youth Project and Brokentalkers (May 2016), who have collectively given permission for the work to be repro-duced here (© Fiona Whelan, Rialto Youth Project and Brokentalkers). We also wish to express our gratitude for permission to use the shorter extract from *Natural History of Hope* in Section 3.

This publication is illustrated by Orla Whelan (2017), © Orla Whelan (see www.whaledust.com).

Introduction

Look at the little crazy guy, swaggering down the hall,
he could dance his way to freedom if you don't make
him fall ...[1]

Many of the words and concepts we use in everyday language have the peculiar feature of being ready to hand and easy to use, until the moment we are asked to explain or defend our usage. This is partly because we may not always be fully aware of *how* we are using words that are so familiar that their meaning appears self-evident.[2] 'Democracy' is a good example. When we say a government or organisation *is* democratic, we are most likely also making an evaluative statement – we are implicitly or explicitly expressing a positive appraisal of the government or organisation in question.[3] 'Freedom' can be a troubling word to use for similar reasons. Is there a valid way to distinguish between the use and misuse of a word such as freedom? There is an extensive and interesting academic literature that can assist us in this regard, for example by enabling us to distinguish freedom *from* (tyranny or domination), freedom *to* (pursue a particular conception of the good life or the good society), and freedom *as* (self-determination or autonomy).[4] If we take the time to study exemplary texts written by philosophers and social scientists on the topic of freedom, then we can learn to grasp – in our mind – the *idea* of freedom. However, this way of knowing is not always satisfactory, not least because many of the great minds who have written on the topic of freedom have done so by retreating from the messiness of the real world in order to construct a purified and unified concept or theory.[5] If we instead begin with a question such as: 'what is it that motivates people to act and struggle in the name of freedom?', then we are perhaps obliged to pay attention to the substance of freedom. In other words, freedom is something we *experience* and *practise* in everyday life.

Freedom is also something we can imagine, but this is arguably different from engaging in theoretical abstraction. To imagine freedom is not the same as being able to debate the work of eminent philosophers on the topic of freedom. To imagine is to imbue our thoughts, and possibly our actions, with the power of creativity; it is to begin to sense that the world we inhabit can be altered, maybe even transformed. This might also serve as a reminder that freedom has a fugitive quality in that it always promises to be more than it actually is. To phrase that slightly differently, to imagine freedom is to reach for something that doesn't exist in the ways in which we might imagine it, and yet does exist to the extent that we can and do experience degrees of freedom in our everyday lives. Does it matter whether we practise and experience *this* type of freedom as opposed to some other imaginable freedom? We think it does matter, which is in part what this book is about.

In contemporary Ireland we are free to participate in what has been described in a series of policy frameworks and economic strategies as the 'knowledge economy'. Predating the sweeping austerity programme that commenced in 2008, it remains a curious feature of the times we live in that the policies which have failed in the past are expected to somehow rise to the challenges of the future. Hence, as talk of economic recovery gains traction, so the idea of a 'knowledge-based and innovation-intensive' economy is again becoming an audible mantra.[6] It is worth recalling that at the height of the boom once known as the Celtic Tiger economy, commentators began using the phrase 'Ireland Inc.', and not always in an ironic sense, which was both instructive and troubling. Tuning into this language as it circulates in the form of spoken and written words, it is all but impossible to miss repeated references to 'innovation and enterprise', two words that follow each other as though joined by an invisible cord. In the language of bloggers and social-media enthusiasts, the innovation/enterprise couplet has gone viral and, as with 'freedom' and 'democracy', these are words that have consequences in terms of how we use them. To take the notion of 'Ireland Inc.' seriously is to assume that democracy has somehow morphed into an enterprise, and insofar as we are free, we are free to innovate and manage ourselves *as* enterprises. We will be using the phrase Enterprise Society as shorthand for this set of issues.[7] This will take some explaining, but for now perhaps we should pause to reflect on the degrees of freedom available to us in the Enterprise Society: we are free to consume – for those who can afford it, and for the rest the alternative is to become enslaved to debt; we are free to choose – from numerous drop-down menus with the available options chosen for us; we are free to compete – making cooperation and solidarity a liability; and we are free to fail – as individuals, meaning that each must take ownership of their own misfortune. However, we are also free to refuse to live on these terms. If we can reimagine freedom, then we can also find ways to do things differently. This is also what this book is about.

A Summary of the Contents

As outlined in the Acknowledgements, Two Fuse is a platform that brings Kevin Ryan and Fiona Whelan together through a commitment to thinking across the boundaries of disciplinary enclosures while also acknowledging the collaborative nature of inquiry. Both of these considerations have a bearing on the internal organisation of the book, which is in four sections. Section 1 is titled 'Degrees of Freedom', and the aim here is to begin to add flesh to the idea of the Enterprise Society by reflecting on how the practice of freedom is conditioned and constrained by visible, intangible and invisible forms of power. Sections 2 and 3 span three fields of practice: sport, academia and art. Section 2, titled

'Freedom in the Enterprise Society: catch up, keep up, get ahead...' is a comparative analysis of two of these fields: high-performance sport, with a focus on professional cycling, and academia. At first glance these fields might seem to have little in common outside of sports-science and sports-studies programmes. However, there are less obvious ways in which these fields of practice are beginning to shade into each other. In France, one of the historical strongholds of sports cycling, road racers were once known as 'pedal workers' because making a living from the sport was understood to be hard manual labour. Things have since changed, of course, and now top-tier professional cyclists live the lives of wealthy celebrities (though they are still the poor cousins of peers in more lucrative sports, such as soccer and tennis). Many more, however, only dream of reaching the top, and the things they do in order to rise up the rankings, or in some cases merely to stay in the sport, can tell us much about the ways in which competition in the more general sense is intensifying. One manifestation of this is the use of performance-enhancing drugs, a contentious issue that affords insight into the excesses of ceaseless innovation. For example, it is not unusual for aspiring young cyclists to pay their own wages in exchange for a chance to race for a professional squad, so that their status as a 'professional' masks the reality of working as an unpaid intern. In the case of seasoned professionals, the terms of employment are typically short contracts of one to three years in duration – which is essentially a form of on-demand labour – a practice that is becoming common in other fields, too, including higher education. Academia produces its own stars – intellectuals who acquire celebrity status[8] – but, as with professional sport, many more struggle to stay in the game and academia is increasingly in step with the wider trend towards flexible and precarious labour. This generates practices which are analogous to performance enhancement in the sporting arena. If professional cycling was once perceived as an exploitative form of manual work and academia an exemplary and prestigious form of mental work, then both have now become a type of machine powered by the excesses of the Enterprise Society. To juxtapose these two fields is to see something of how the practice of freedom is shaped by the pressure to excel, the imperative to do whatever it takes to keep up with one's peers and rivals, and the opportunity to fail.

The field of art is by no means immune to these trends; indeed, a growing emphasis on the economic potential of the 'cultural and creative industries' might be taken as an indication of the extent to which art is becoming yet another enterprise.[9] However, many artists are working at or beyond the fringes of the culture industry and some push beyond the boundaries of art itself so that art becomes a form of social practice. This is why we turn to the field of art in Section 3, which is titled 'Reimagining the Practice of Freedom'. Presented as a dialogue, our conversation focuses on *collaborative* and socially *engaged* practice, that is, artistic processes and projects concerned with social issues and/or political change, orchestrated through meaningful engagement with people, and typically manifesting beyond the confines of galleries, museums and festivals. More specifically, we discuss Fiona's collaborative art practice, which is based in Dublin and spans more than a decade, exploring and addressing power relations through durational, reciprocal engagements with people and place. It is important to make this connection between power and freedom explicit from the outset. We will be focusing on how the practice of freedom is shaped and formed by power, and in different ways, so that power constrains but may also enhance or transform the practice of freedom. In short, power and freedom are inextricably linked, which is why we will have much to say about power in this book. In addition, and as noted above, there is nothing intrinsic to the field of art that sets it apart as a privileged site from where alternatives to the Enterprise Society might emerge. Insofar as alternatives are possible, these will have to emerge within spaces sometimes described as 'interstices' – spaces *between* aesthetics and politics to be opened out from within the tissue and texture of social life itself. In this way we also hope to respond to the aims of the *Síreacht* series, and here it might be worth recalling a slogan born from the tumultuous events of May 1968 in Paris: 'Sous les pavés, la plage!' ('Under the cobblestones, the beach!').[10] Another world is always possible, but first we must be able to imagine it.

It was never our intention to write a conventional conclusion to this book, which is why we have framed freedom as a question in the title. Freedom is as much problem as practice, and to try to reach a conclusion as to what freedom *is* or *ought to be* would be an exercise in folly, because it would be like trying to harness or shackle the imaginable. In place of a conclusion, we are instead writing towards a transitional point, and thus in the final section (Section 4) we present extracts from a public performance called *Natural History of Hope* (Fiona Whelan, Rialto Youth Project, and Brokentalkers, 2016). This is discussed in detail in Section 3; for now it is enough to point out that this way of ending the book is intended as an invitation to others to join us in exploring the possibility of reimagining the practice of freedom.

Sections 1–4 might be described as a set of cumulative steps. The first step gathers together the tools to be used for critical inquiry, the second step conducts a type of diagnostics, and the third and fourth steps explore the possibility of breaching the constraints of the Enterprise Society. Imagine yourself working at a computer and it starts to do odd things; it's not broken exactly, but it's glitchy to the point where it stops being a useful tool and starts to become a stress-inducing hindrance. Someone who knows their way around the computer's operating system can probably put their finger on the problem, even if they don't necessarily know how to fix it. This is essentially what Section 2 attempts to do. By examining recent developments that traverse the fields of high-performance sport and academia, we attempt to show how comparative analysis can yield insights of more general relevance, in effect constructing a portrait of freedom as practised in the Enterprise Society. This type of diagnostics reaches its limits, however, at the point where it runs up against the question of what comes next. We have no satisfactory answer to that question, but we are keen to explore it through dialogue. There is something of an invisible boundary that often separates academic inquiry from the world of practice, exemplifying a more general tendency to partition the social world along the contours of specialisation, in turn giving rise to enclosures of knowledge. By engaging in dialogue (Section 3) that crosses this invisible boundary, our aim is to approach freedom as a question and to use dialogue as a way of keeping this question open, thereby avoiding the temptation to close it down. In other words, we are not writing towards a terminus where we claim to have answered or resolved our question (as in: The End), and we will not be presenting a fictional Utopia or hypothetical account of life after the Enterprise Society (whatever that might look like). Instead, our objective is to learn from what people are actually doing as they engage with the ways in which power both constrains and augments the practice of freedom.

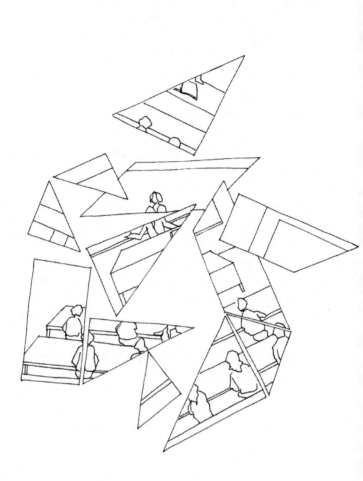

Degrees of Freedom

In the introduction we have made a case for approaching freedom not as an abstract figure of thought, but rather as a tangible feature of everyday life. Freedom is something we experience and something we do, but it is also something we have learnt to do – a set of acquired skills and competencies anchored in the manifold situations and contexts of everyday social life – and in this sense freedom is a cultural practice. Moreover, in suggesting that the practice of freedom is a matter of degree, we have implied something that needs to be examined in more depth: the ways in which power conditions and constrains the practice of freedom. In this section we use the relation between power and freedom as a line of approach to the Enterprise Society, thereby adding texture to the initial sketch of this idea as presented in the introduction.

As with the concept of freedom, there is a voluminous academic literature on power that offers different – and at times competing – perspectives, theories and definitions.[11]

In order to stay focused on the task at hand, we will not be surveying this literature but instead using it to contrast visible and invisible power.[12] By visible power we mean power that is attached to offices of the state or the boardroom or the classroom; power that is invested in authority, such as a government or regulatory body, and power as codified in the form of laws and rules. We are subject to the rule of law as citizens or denizens and we are also routinely governed by rules and regulations, whether in the workplace, at school, or in a sports club or civil-society organisation. In these situations we generally have a fairly good idea of what to expect in the way of sanctions or penalties if we break the law or breach the rules. However, these same constraints also bestow us with rights and agency, and in this sense they may augment our freedom. We might, for example, contest the exercise of power if we feel we have been treated unfairly, or if we believe those in authority have abused the power they wield over us and/or others. Visible power is arguably most visible when resisted or contested, for example when people take to the streets to protest knowing they risk violent confrontation with police. Yet even when it goes uncontested or, indeed, unnoticed – somewhat similar to ambient noise – this mode of power is still in plain sight.

To move away from the most visible forms of power is to encounter less tangible constraints, often referred to as norms.[13] There is the question of whether the concept of power is stretched too far if used to encompass this type of constraint, and we address that issue a little later with the help of an example. For now it might be noted that there is at least one significant difference between a formal rule and a social norm: the latter rarely exists in the way a legal statute or rule book exists. This less tangible form of power might be characterised as the constraints of sociality and belonging, whether at the macro level of cultural identity (such as ethnicity or religion) or the micro level of social circles (family and friends). In between are place-based communities such as neighbourhoods and communities of interest like sports clubs and civil-society organisations. Note that this repetition of examples (sports club and civil-society organisation) is intended to emphasise the ways in which visible power can shade into less tangible forms of power. In other words, in contrasting visible and intangible power, we are not suggesting distinct social realms. If we choose not to drive whilst drunk, is it because we act on the basis of moral principles (we do not wish to endanger the lives of others), because we respect or fear the law, or because we may be shamed in front of family and friends if stopped and breathalysed? Such questions are not always easy to answer because the well springs of our actions may be a blend of legal and social constraints a well as principled reasons. This complexity becomes particularly acute when invisible power enters the frame of analysis.

In order to unpack this notion of invisible power, it is helpful to return to the concept of a cultural practice, noting that this is more than merely the doing of something. A cultural practice is an extensive stock of practical know-how, which is by no means static or unchanging, yet still relatively durable. For the purpose of explication, it can also be approached at different scales or levels of analysis. At the macro level of population groups, a cultural practice emerges gradually through the interweaving of visible and intangible forms of power, and can thus be examined historically. It is also a type of script which is routinely enacted at the micro level of interpersonal relations. This is not to suggest that we are caged by cultural practices – there are manifold ways of improvising – and we will have more to say about that in due course. For now, in order to clarify the notion of invisible power, we need to attend to how cultural practices shape (and are shaped by) the ways in which we perceive and engage with the world around us, and this in turn has a bearing on how we live our lives, both as individuals and collectively. This is crucially important, because when we think and act in a particular way we foreclose on other possible ways of living our lives. To grasp this insight is to view one's self and also the world one inhabits through the lens of *contingency*: who we are as individuals, what we are as a society or a people, could be otherwise.[14] Perhaps the best way to approach invisible power is through examples, which will also serve to clarify how this differs from – but also relates to – visible and intangible forms of power. We start with an example that brings history into play, followed by a second example that focuses squarely on how practical know-how conditions the practice of freedom. The two examples will also combine as a lens through which to examine freedom in the Enterprise Society.

The first example begins with something so common-place that it hardly warrants a second thought – something most of us (there are always exceptions) will remember doing as young children, and something we did so often that at some point it became habitual – sitting in our appointed place in a classroom. There is rarely any need to question something so ordinary, and it is only in the context of disruptive behaviour that the rule governing this way of doing things becomes visible. Some children are docile and compliant within the classroom setting, while others are more unruly and need to be coaxed and warned by the teacher before they settle into the lesson. Yet, despite variations that might distinguish one classroom from another – the ways in which particular groups of children generate very specific dynamics, the ethos adopted by individual schools, the extent to which a given school is adequately or inadequately resourced, and so on – education is a field of practice that moves to the rhythm of the clock and the calendar. The field of education is governed as much by patterned behaviour as it is by the visible power of statutes, government departments and boards of management. From Monday to Friday, for the duration of the school year, approximately one million primary and secondary schoolchildren in the Republic of Ireland enter the classroom and take their appointed place.[15] Who invented this practice?

The short answer is nobody, or rather, no single person. As with cultural practices more generally, the machinery of mass education came into existence gradually, from roughly the end of the eighteenth century onwards, and was born from a whole variety of social experiments on the part of educationalists, philanthropists, religious organisations and various branches of the state.[16] There isn't space here to do more than sketch an outline of this history, and thus the discussion will be confined to a few general observations about the *what* and *why* of these experiments. Notwithstanding the sheer variety of methods employed, one of the central concerns was trying to work out the most efficient and effective way of teaching a large group of students, which in essence was a problem of discipline. Important, too, is the fact that the main target of these experiments were the children of the poor.[17] In the context of accelerating industrialisation and urbanisation, poor children became the focus of visible power, partly because they were becoming more visible as they congregated on the streets of rapidly expanding towns and cities, but also because they were *made* visible in a very specific way. For example, the nineteenth century saw the emergence of what were known as 'statistical societies' in Britain and Ireland, forums where the objectivity of scientific method was to serve as a bulwark against the partisan nature of party politics.[18] When the upstanding members of these societies met to present their research to each other – people such as William Nielson Hancock, who was Whately Chair of Political Economy in Trinity College,

Dublin from 1846 to 1851, and president of the Statistical and Social Inquiry Society of Ireland from 1881 to 1882 – they conversed in the language of facts. For example, when Hancock presented a paper on 'The Feasibility of Compulsory Education in Ireland' to the Statistical Society, London in 1879, his argument was bolstered by what at the time were known as 'moral' statistics, and the statistics stated that compulsory education was an effective way of reducing crime.[19]

Mary Carpenter was another mid-nineteenth-century philanthropist and social reformer who campaigned tirelessly on behalf of the children of the poor. The daughter of a Unitarian minister, Carpenter co-founded a 'ragged school' – a free school for poor children – in her home city of Bristol, and her book on *Reformatory Schools for the Children of the Perishing and Dangerous Classes*[20] was instrumental in establishing a parliamentary investigation into juvenile delinquency in 1852. Similar to Hancock, Carpenter's argument was that it was imperative to 'rescue' the 'children of the perishing and dangerous classes' from parental 'neglect', meaning what was, in her eyes, inadequate parenting.[21] The twin ideas of 'neglect' and 'rescue' combined as a technique that – even if not described in this way at the time – attempted to thread visible, intangible and invisible power together. At the heart of the problem of the perishing and dangerous classes was norm-regulated behaviour. Reformers such as Carpenter were of the opinion that the children of the poor were being steered by norms that placed them on the road to crime and vice, and this was to be countered by a reformatory influence that would train them in the habits of a 'moral' life. Once norm-regulated behaviour is conceived in this way, that is – as something that can be acted upon with a view to training minds and bodies – then it becomes an intricate form of power. The children to be rescued in this way were first to be subject to visible power by taking them from the family home, thereby placing them in residential schools where they would undergo a process of character reformation, later to be released back into society as industrious workers and law-abiding citizens. Along the way power was to become invisible, embodied as habits of virtuous thought and moral action (or at least that was the theory). Even as support for mass compulsory education began to gain traction, so this type of experiment in preventive education laid the groundwork for a system of industrial and reformatory schools.[22]

This is not to suggest that children are simply moulded by power and slotted into their designated places in the social order, but neither should we forget that a whole set of ancillary practices gradually came into existence to supplement day schools, by monitoring the homes of the poor and managing children deemed to be deviant and recalcitrant.[23] These included not only industrial schools and reformatory schools – and by the end of the nineteenth century these were populated by thousands of children – but also juvenile courts and prisons, professional social work, and forms of physical and psychiatric evaluation such as school medical inspections. To thread these instruments and techniques together is to see something of how the practice of freedom is conditioned by constraints that span visible, intangible and invisible power. To reiterate a point made in the introduction: power and freedom are inextricably linked.

As noted above, one of the main difficulties encountered on the way to instituting mass education was the problem of discipline. The children of the poor were unaccustomed to exercising the kind of obedient self-restraint expected of them in the classroom. Arranging children in an orderly grid of desks and benches, with each child facing the teacher, was a mode of control. Not only would this ensure that each child could follow the lesson, it was also a way of keeping each child and the class as a whole under surveillance. From its inception, mass education was to function as a machine to instil *self-discipline*. The physical arrangement of bodies in space operated in conjunction with the repetitive routine of the timetable, with the school day broken up into modular segments devoted to specific lessons and activities.[24] Time itself was disciplined through the use of bells or a sharp clap of the hands on the part of teachers, forms of sonic power that signalled the end of one activity and the start of the next.

During the twentieth century, compulsory education up to a specified age became a legally codified right. Moreover, mass education became increasingly standardised and was administered directly and indirectly by the state, the latter being the case in Ireland, with religious organisations playing a major role in the field of education. Although we – as a society – routinely quarrel over how best to manage and administer primary, secondary and higher education, and though we may dispute the purpose of education, this is merely the surface level of a practice that is deeply embedded in the institutional and ideational fabric of society. Something as simple as children routinely sitting at their appointed place in the classroom helps to reproduce this vast edifice. The point to be stressed here is that doing a history of cultural practices is a bit like trying to build a puzzle from pieces that do not fit neatly together in the way one might expect them to. A cultural practice is more like an accident than a design: something that comes into existence gradually and haphazardly, shaped by numerous actions and intentions, and with nobody in total control. Furthermore, what starts out as visible power gradually becomes the intangible power of norm-regulated constraints, finally becoming an invisible stock of shared practical know-how.

Now framed as a right,[25] education is closely related to freedom in that it has become *the* gateway and pathway to opportunity while also being *the* solution to poverty, inequality and exclusion. However, it could be argued that while many educational practices operating within schools have changed, schools still function in pretty much the same way they did during the nineteenth century. The visible power of *compulsory* education has gradually dropped out of sight, yet schools are still instruments of power, which leads to our second example: the notion of 'disadvantage'. This has all but eclipsed other more conflictual ways of framing inequality, such as 'labour exploitation', 'structures of oppression', or 'institutionalised racism'. The concept of disadvantage has reshaped the meaning of inequality by equating this primarily with employability, in turn helping to instrumentalise education.[26]

An example from Ireland is a policy document titled *A Programme for a Partnership Government*, published in May 2016.[27] Pledging to 'build a strong economy and to deliver a fair society' (note the order of priorities), the *Programme* outlines a series of measures to deal with 'disadvantaged communities', 'disadvantaged urban areas', 'educational disadvantage' and 'disadvantaged children'. In terms of how the partnership government plans to 'tackle disadvantage', the emphasis falls squarely on 'skills and employability'. As was the case during the time of Hancock and Carpenter, education is posited as the solution to poverty, crime and welfare dependency, and as a response to inequality, the aim is to equip the poor and the excluded to play the game of enterprise and innovation, even if this means compelling them to do so by making welfare stingier and the penal system harsher.[28] Tackling disadvantage means making sure that children are job-ready and ensuring that working-age adults take charge of their own employability, or in the case of the poor, their own misfortune. Furthermore, as a way of governing inequality, this also revives a much older way of blaming the poor for their poverty by distinguishing the 'deserving' from the 'underserving' poor. In other words, if some among us refuse or fail to avail of the opportunities to become employable, then perhaps they deserve to be disadvantaged.[29]

Disadvantage has become a type of meta-narrative that frames poverty and exclusion as the unfortunate by-product of globalisation. To *be* disadvantaged is to be *at* a disadvantage relative to others, and thus the solution is to enable the disadvantaged to catch up, keep pace and get ahead. Disadvantage is like a story that begins with a lament and ends in a race, and it goes something like this: 'It is terribly unfortunate that some people are poor or excluded, but nobody is to blame for this situation, and redistributing wealth from rich to poor will only exacerbate the problem by penalising those who contribute most to the economy. The only effective policy is to help the disadvantaged to help themselves – to enable them to compete for jobs and thereby achieve financial independence.' 'Disadvantage' is made practical in ways that span visible and invisible forms of power, and like silt that sediments on a riverbed and gradually becomes solid, it settles into our practical know-how and becomes part of the bedrock of social relations.

As the million children mentioned above make their way through the various tiers of the Irish education system – some exiting in second level, many continuing to higher education – they are schooled in the ethos of innovation and enterprise, and not necessarily by teachers or the content of the curriculum. Children are schooled in many ways – commonly described as a process of socialisation – and the practicalities of meeting the demands of a deeply competitive educational system (or from the perspective of parents, the challenge of securing a good education for one's child) can be mapped onto the narrative of (dis)advantage: catch up, keep up, get ahead. Schools and scholars are pressured to find ways to gain the edge in situations where exam results, school league tables and university rankings have concrete consequences. When university students opt to buy an essay from an internet-based provider such as Rush Essay[30] – a service that offers clients 'custom essays guaranteed to be plagiarism-free' – it is perhaps too simplistic to equate this with cheating, and one way of pulling back from the urge to do so is to reverse the lens so that we see who writes these on-demand custom essays. Using the pseudonym 'Ed Dante', one such ghost-writer told his story for *The Chronicle Review of Higher Education* in 2010.[31] Describing himself as a 'hired gun, a doctor of everything, an academic mercenary', Ed Dante claimed to be highly qualified having 'written towards' a master's degree in cognitive psychology and a PhD in sociology, and he also claimed he was earning more money than many of his peers struggling to make ends meet as educators. Many full-time third-level students are also struggling – to hold down a job, care for family members, or cope with serious personal issues – and the decision to be innovative in keeping pace with the challenges of a degree programme may not always be taken lightly. This issue is examined in more detail in the next section under the heading of performance enhancement; suffice for now to note that this is one of the excesses generated by the Enterprise Society.

Whatever about the Irish government's somewhat fuzzy commitment to a fair society, the reality is that in the Enterprise Society large numbers of people make ends meet by freelancing – people like Ed Dante – and many of these people are university and college graduates, people who might well expect to be advantaged rather than disadvantaged. The gig economy, also known as 'platform capitalism', exemplifies the life of a freelancing entrepreneur.[32] If you are a versatile and efficient writer, you can acquire gigs of the Ed Dante variety; if you have a car you can find work as a driver through Uber; if you have a house or an apartment you can find paying guests via Airbnb; if you have skills and tools you can find clients through TaskRabbit, and if all you have is a willingness to supply on-demand labour, there are opportunities to acquire cleaning gigs or shopping gigs, such as buying and delivering groceries through platforms like Instacart. Though still in its infancy in Ireland, the international trend suggests that this is the shape of things to come. The basic idea is that anyone with a smartphone and the requisite app can become an entrepreneur. Indeed, the empowering potential of the gig economy has received much hype; freelancing is becoming a form of freedom to be embraced, because it means YOU are in control. But who exactly is in control, and of what? Freelance gigs can be used to supplement income from a regular job, but the gig economy is also bidding down the value of labour because it is costed in a very different way: no sick pay, no holiday pay, no pension entitlements and no parental leave. For those entirely reliant on gig-related income, entrepreneurship may well serve as an alibi for a stressful and precarious life.[33] Internships, too, are a burgeoning trend and, again, there is a clear tension between the idea that internships are empowering and the argument that they are deeply exploitative.[34] In some cases internships are a transitional step with real prospects of a decent wage and/or fulfilling work; in other cases they amount to a treadmill of unpaid or underpaid labour, with one internship leading to another. The Irish state's National Internship Scheme – called JobBridge, offering welfare recipients work-placement opportunities – is a case in point. Recently axed following an external review (the minister for social protection has announced that it is to be replaced with a 'more targeted work experience programme in 2017'[35]), JobBridge was mired in scandal in 2014 when it transpired that schools were using the scheme to offset the cost of cleaners and caretakers.[36] This is yet another manifestation of on-demand labour, because these particular internships last for nine months, the same length of time as the second-level school year.

The more we rely on the story of disadvantage as a way of understanding inequality, the harder it is to grasp the ways in which the Enterprise Society itself is the source of social suffering, or the extent to which zero-sum games of enterprise and innovation generate situations where the lives of many are diminished. In short, the Enterprise Society is powered by inequality, and the kind of equal opportunity on offer is the opportunity to rise or fall by engaging in ceaseless competition.[37] Precarious and poorly paid work has become a normal feature of everyday life for many people in the Enterprise Society. If the notion of disadvantage obscures, rather than clarifies, our understanding of inequality, then perhaps we need new words or a new language to enable us to rethink and re-perceive equality and, from there, to imagine a better world.

There are many ways in which we are compelled to play the game of enterprise, because there are consequences attached to playing badly or refusing to play at all. But what about the ways in which we *willingly* participate? Some no doubt thrive on competition, but is there any reason why success or the pursuit of excellence should be a zero-sum game of winning and losing? Perhaps the larger problem is that we haven't yet figured out how not to succumb to the constraints of the Enterprise Society, and before we can even begin to open out that question, we need to try to understand something of how we are complicit in this scripted practice of freedom. This is the task of the next section, which presents a comparative analysis of high-performance sport and academia. The question explored in the next section is this: if being advantaged is the answer to disadvantage, then how do we go about the business of catching up, keeping up and getting ahead. The emphasis will be on the 'how', thus focusing on practice, on the routine and often banal ways in which athletes and academics play the game of innovation and enterprise, and in so doing become both the instrument and target of visible, intangible and invisible power.

It might be pointed out that a more effective way of critiquing the Enterprise Society would be to focus on those who are framed by the concept of disadvantage (the poor, the excluded, the marginalised). We will get to that in due course, but first we want to examine how freedom in the Enterprise Society is becoming a race without a finishing line.

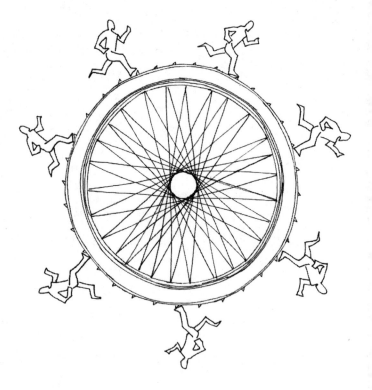

Freedom in the Enterprise Society: catch up, keep up, get ahead ...

I n her book *Academic Freedom in an Age of Conformity*, Joanna Williams argues that:

> Freedom to propose the outrageous and challenge the ordinary is as essential for individual liberty as it is for society's collective knowledge and understanding of the world to advance. This understanding – that personal freedom is a prerequisite for both a critique of conventional knowledge and the search for the new – was established over two centuries ago.[38]

Williams is referring specifically to the German philosopher Emmanuel Kant who, in 1784, wrote about enlightenment as 'freedom to make public use of one's reason in all matters'. Kant thus becomes a cardinal reference point in the history of academic freedom, which passes through the mid-nineteenth-century writings of John Stuart Mill ('Genius can only breathe freely in an atmosphere of freedom') to Albert Einstein, who, having fled Nazi Germany in 1933, delivered a speech in London on the theme of 'Science and Civilisation', in which he argued that 'intellectual and individual freedom' is the source of advances in 'knowledge and invention'.[39]

The aim of Williams' journey into the past is partly to provide evidence of historical continuity. Although the meaning of academic freedom is hotly debated today, there is nevertheless an enduring set of values that pivot around the 'freedom to propose the outrageous and challenge the ordinary'. In tracing this history Williams also presents an understanding of academic freedom derived from liberalism, which is made concrete when she invokes the metaphor of a 'marketplace of ideas'.[40] Just as 'rational consumers freely choose the best products having considered issues of price, quality and relevance to their needs', argues Williams, so 'intellectually autonomous individuals' should be free to choose from a range of ideas and truth claims, because only in this way do we ensure that ideas enter into competition with each other. Knowledge ought to be contestable, says Williams, and we have no disagreement with her on this point. However, to assume that 'the advantage of a marketplace of ideas is that the best, least refutable, ideas will win out no matter how often they are contested or by whom' seems dangerously naive. Markets are never free, and the marketplace of ideas is conditioned and constrained by visible and invisible forms of power.[41] Indeed, it could be argued that Williams is engaging with the Enterprise Society on its own terms by using the metaphor of a marketplace. Furthermore, though on one level Williams is discussing something very specific – academic freedom – she is also constructing a more encompassing theory of freedom per se. Derived from the tradition of liberal political thought, and modelled on the competitive logic of markets, this is presented as though its efficacy and desirability are self-evident – and to a greater or lesser extent they are – but in our view this is precisely the problem. In the context of the Enterprise Society, this way of picturing freedom has become like Teflon, in that it is highly resistant to critique, yet at root it remains both contingent and contestable.

We are not suggesting that Williams is entirely off the mark – we are broadly in agreement with the strand of her argument that insists on the importance of challenging ideas that take on the character of unquestionable truth – but her way of framing the problem perhaps misses something important and, again, this necessitates attention to practice. The practice of freedom within (and indeed beyond) the field of academia is increasingly steered by *a specific type of competition* that extends from individual lecturers and researchers to universities competing for inward investment and market share. We also need to look closely at how the (once?) radical idea of 'challenging the ordinary' has been captured by the language of 'innovation and enterprise', and we need to examine how the pursuit of excellence is a contest whereby each and all are enjoined to excel by exceeding the performance of peers and rivals. The stakes are high, because this is a game of success and failure which is played to the tune of 'transparency and accountability' (more on that shortly). It is by no means clear how comparing freedom to a marketplace can do anything other than reinforce the growing inequalities generated by the Enterprise Society.[42]

Let us begin then with the most visible forms of power currently shaping the field of academia. Higher education in Ireland, as elsewhere, is being reconfigured through programmes of reform variously referred to as the new public management, new managerialism and performance management – practices developed in the private sector and now being used to 'modernise' the public sector.[43] The substance of these practices entails the use of instruments and technologies that seek to make actions and outputs visible and verifiable by measuring and incentivising performance through various types of audit as well as flexible or 'atypical' labour contracts.[44] Powerful ideas such as 'accountability' – powerful because these are difficult to critique without inviting suspicion – are driving this process, which is harnessed to strategic objectives such as delivering value for money by rewarding effort and weeding out waste. Another driver is quality assurance. In Europe, quality assurance is built into the Bologna Process for cooperation in higher education, the aim of which is to establish a European Higher Education Area.[45]

The European Association for Quality Assurance in Higher Education (ENQA) is the umbrella organisation for Bologna signatory countries, and in its mission statement ENQA states that it is committed to 'the enhancement of quality and the development of a quality culture in higher education'.[46] To cut through the rhetoric, Bologna is a coordinated strategy to place higher education in the service of economic growth and global competitiveness. Though the strategy is framed as one of cooperation, quality is one of the ways in which higher-education institutions compete for market share by developing distinct brands and unique products. In short, the new managerialism and quality assurance combine in instituting an enterprise culture that connects public entities (universities) to commercial interests (discussed below). Moreover, there is a type of symmetry between those who manage and monitor others and those who self-manage. On one side is a drive to govern through quality review and evaluative monitoring on the part of policy-makers and university-management teams, which has the effect, whether intended or not, of routinising surveillance and suspicion.[47] On the other side is self-surveillance, practised by researchers striving to enhance impact and reputation by making effort and achievement as visible as possible. We also want to examine how rivalry between institutions and among individuals is leveraged by for-profit actors that exploit the open-access movement. In engaging with this weave of visible, intangible and invisible power, we will be carving out a slightly elliptical path, re-approaching academia via the arena of high-performance sport, which will help to illuminate key features of the Enterprise Society.

Innovation and Counter-Innovation: The 'arms race' of performance enhancement

Over the past twenty years or so, the credibility of professional sport has been continually undermined by a series of 'doping' scandals relating to the use of prohibited performance-enhancing drugs (PEDs). In some cases this is attributed to unethical behaviour on the part of individuals, while in other cases it is orchestrated on a much larger scale. A recent inquiry into state-sponsored doping in Russia, for example, extends to approximately one thousand athletes across thirty sports.[48] There is nothing new about athletes using drugs to gain the competitive edge, but it does seem that the issue of doping in sport has become increasingly politicised over time.[49] It is also the case that the practice of doping itself has shifted, from the use of pain-suppressants and stimulants such as amphetamine, to more sophisticated drugs like erythropoietin (EPO). Developed as an anti-anaemic drug to treat renal failure, AIDS and cancer, EPO is used in sport to boost the production of red blood cells, in effect enriching the body's 'fuel' by delivering more oxygen to the muscles. In the sport of cycling for example, EPO enables athletes to train harder and recover faster, thereby enhancing performance in ways that go well beyond the gains achieved through the use of drugs like amphetamines. Furthermore, it took years to develop a test for EPO, and when a test did eventually become available, the response was to adapt by innovating: instead of injecting EPO, athletes switched to 'blood doping' (blood transfusions, another way of increasing the volume of red blood cells). This ongoing contest – between innovation in the use of PEDs and counter-innovation on the part of anti-doping agencies – has been described by some analysts as an 'arms race'.[50] We want to suggest that this contest is something like the pulse of the Enterprise Society.

The sport of cycling has long been at the epicentre of this cycle of innovation and counter-innovation. The Tour de France is the most prestigious event in the world of professional cycling, and in 2010 on the eve of the *Grand Départ* (a phrase traditionally used to announce the start of this iconic race, which lasts for three full weeks), the world governing body of sports cycling – the Union Cycliste Internationale (UCI) – created an 'index of suspicion'. All 198 riders taking part in the race were assigned a number between one and ten, with a score of six or higher signalling an 'overwhelming' possibility of doping.[51] This is indicative of the extent to which anti-doping agencies are looking increasingly to innovations in the field of information technology as a means of developing tools for detection and deterrence, which is also what enabled the UCI to construct its index of suspicion. Each rider's score was based on their Biological Passport, which is an electronic document that records a haematological and steroid profile of the individual athlete derived from test results (blood and urine). Testing is conducted both during competition and out of competition, and the latest World Anti-Doping Code (published by the World Anti-Doping Agency in 2015) stipulates that athletes can be tested anywhere, at any time (day or night), by any anti-doping agency with authority over the athlete.[52] To ensure that this policy can be implemented, athletes in the testing pool are required to file 'whereabouts' reports with the relevant anti-doping authority, thereby making themselves available for one hour every day, seven days a week, between the hours of 6.00 a.m. and 11.00 p.m. A notable feature of this apparatus is that it renders everyone a suspect whilst also making suspicion actionable. All athletes are potential dopers and blanket surveillance lays the groundwork for targeted action in the case of a red flag. Further to this, an athlete can be sanctioned on the basis of anti-doping-rule violations, such as inaccurate whereabouts information, as well as 'adverse analytical findings' and 'atypical passport findings'. In other words, athletes can be punished without ever testing positive for a banned substance. Another significant feature of this apparatus is that it violates rights to privacy by instituting intrusive forms of surveillance that would not normally be tolerated outside of prisons and the military.[53] What is thus so surprising is the lack of resistance on the part of athletes.[54]

A case in point is the British/Kenyan cyclist, Christopher Froome. Froome won his first Tour de France in 2013, and such was his dominance in the high mountains (where the race is typically won or lost) that rumours quickly spread alleging he was using PEDs. Judged guilty in the mass-mediated court of public opinion, Froome's response was to stage a counter-attack by making a slice of his physiological data available for independent analysis.[55] More recently, having won the Tour de France for a second time in 2015 and again facing allegations of doping, Froome announced his intention to undertake a series of independent tests at key points during the racing season so that his data could be mapped longitudinally, with the results made available publicly.[56] Froome's response to accusations of cheating has thus been to demand more intrusive surveillance on top of what is already considered by many to be an invasive anti-doping-testing regime. Perhaps of more relevance here, however, is what this reveals about the liberal ideal of meritocracy: if the rewards of sporting success and athletic achievement are to be distributed on the basis of merit, then each must be free to compete on equal terms with all, and if this is to be the case, then the scope of freedom must be subject to controls. Even before exploring any further, we see freedom becoming entwined with power.

Another point the doping issue underscores is that the visible power of rules and sanctions is either reinforced or thwarted by the intangible power of norm-regulated behaviour, that is, as riders move up the various tiers of the sport and enter the ranks of professional cycling, they experience peer pressure that either draws them towards the arts of doping or steers them clear of it.[57] The historical record indicates that many riders who dope do so because they come to see this as being a normal – albeit illegal – part of the job, like shaving their legs and making sure they eat and drink enough during a race. Hence, associations such as the Mouvement Pour un Cyclisme Crédible are trying to orchestrate cultural change within the sport, the idea being that racing clean can and should become the new normal.[58] This is comparable to the techniques employed by nineteenth-century reformers as discussed earlier: implant new habits of thought and action into those at risk of being lured into a life of crime and vice. Whether through visible or intangible power, the objective is basically the same: to act upon the athlete's actions, so that making the 'right' choice becomes an act of individual volition. This makes for quite a contrast when compared to the idea – popular among many political theorists – that freedom is the absence of external interference. Here we have different attempts to *produce*, *steer* and *direct* the practice of freedom, and these methods are by no means mutually exclusive.

This cycle of innovation and counter-innovation thus extends from the visible power of surveillance and sanctions to intangible forms of power that attempt to act upon the attitudes, as well as the actions, of athletes. Gradually, much of this becomes invisible power, part of the occupational culture of elite-level sport. Being an elite athlete today is like living in a glass cage; even as athletes with nothing to hide push for greater transparency, so those with something to hide must do likewise in order to remain credible. Credible performance is staged on the terrain of transparency and accountability, but this gives rise to a paradox. Transparency is often invoked by those who champion democracy and stand opposed to the secretive and shadowy power of surveillance, whether wielded by states over citizens or by corporate giants as they harvest and leverage data gathered from credit-card transactions, online activity and so forth. Yet in the world of elite sport, transparency *is* a form of surveillance, while surveillance articulates the virtues of transparency. This somewhat paradoxical situation is by no means peculiar to the field of high-performance sport.

Meritocracy Unbound

Similar to blanket suspicion in the sporting arena, surveillance is becoming a routine feature of academic life, yet there is one important difference. In the case of the athlete, suspicion is aroused when an extraordinary performance exceeds what is deemed humanly possible. In academia, by way of contrast, performance must exceed the norm and to be ranked as average is to be failing. It is in this sense that 'excellence' should be understood, because to excel is to exceed the achievements of others. The experience of this persistent pressure to excel is conveyed extremely well by Stephen Ball (professor of sociology of education at Oxford University) when he writes of accountability in higher education, meaning the ways in which academic labour is subject to a panoply of judgements, measurements, targets and comparisons, leading to:

> ... a sense of being constantly judged in different ways, by different means, according to different criteria, through different agents and agencies. There is a flow of changing demands, expectations and indicators that makes one continually accountable and constantly recorded. We become ... unsure whether we are doing enough, doing the right thing, doing as much as others, or as well as others, constantly looking to improve, to be better, to be excellent.[59]

It is worth pausing here to reflect on the pros, as well as the cons, of performance metrics as a way of rewarding effort and achievement. With respect to the public sector, it has been argued that this is a desirable alternative to past practices when it comes to ranking candidates for promotion, and that as a way of implementing the ideal of meritocracy, performance management is an improvement on practices that reward individuals solely on the basis of seniority and length of service.[60] However (and this complicates Froome's support for intrusive controls as noted above), as a way of defending the ideal of meritocracy, this operates on the basis of naive naturalism. Here the sport/academia analogy is particularly striking. In the sporting arena anti-doping agencies condemn the use of PEDs because this violates the ideal of playing 'clean' and 'true'. It is as though hard work and genetic inheritance set some sort of natural limits to competition, but there are many ways to enhance performance. The sport of cycling, for example, has spawned an industry in research and development, with enormous sums of money invested in clothing and equipment with the aim of saving a few watts of power through reduced wind-drag. In elite-level sport the difference between the best and the rest is measured in terms of marginal gains. A handful of watts can make the difference between winning and coming second, or for jobbing cyclists, between having a contract beyond the current season and having to exit the sport. Factoring in other legal methods of human enhancement – such as nutritional supplements and new training techniques derived from innovations in the field of sports science – in what sense we can speak meaningfully of the un-enhanced athlete is by no means clear.

As this culture of augmentation expands in scope, it also escapes the grip of regulation. In sport, the use of PEDs is regulated by anti-doping agencies, but, as noted by the historian John Hoberman, 'modern societies that run on the principles of productivity and efficiency cannot credibly oppose techniques that boost the human organism in order to enhance its mental, physical and sexual performances'.[61] One such cognitive enhancer is modafinil (Provigil), a wake-fulness drug designed to treat narcolepsy and easily available to buy online. Used to boost productivity and performance, modafinil is reported to be gaining currency in the global academic community, and if one person equates this with cheating, another might see it as a way of gaining the competitive edge.[62] It is also worth noting that the use of 'smart drugs' in academia has been defended on the grounds that they offer the means of 'levelling up'.[63] Whether in sport or academia, natural ability can be enhanced, while success-oriented commitment – willpower, focus and dedication – can also be augmented. In short, the meritocratic ideal of a level playing field belongs to a bygone era. It should be noted that there is at least one important difference between sport and academia, in that academics do not need to fear the equivalent of anti-doping agencies, but in any case we are not suggesting that the use of PEDs in academia is rife. Rather, there is something of a Pandora's box to this, and to delve into it and rummage around is to see something of how the culture of augmentation is happening in more pervasive and mundane ways, enabled by technologies to boost research 'footprint' and impact.

Visibility and the Glass Cage of Academia

Social-networking sites for researchers such as Academia.edu and ResearchGate are on an upward trajectory in terms of users, with both platforms affording a way of becoming more 'Googleable'. Both of these platforms are funded by venture capital, both have emerged in tandem with the open-access movement, and both exhibit more than a passing similarity to Facebook. The number of 'views' or 'reads' on these platforms resembles the number of 'likes' on a Facebook page, while 'followers' mirror Facebook 'friends'. Insofar as this type of visibility helps to boost professional standing, it looks a little like a popularity contest. ResearchGate's RG Score – which is presented as 'a new way to measure scientific reputation' – captures all interactions on the platform, including the reputation of those who download and follow one's work. A big RG Score is thus an indication that one's research is attracting the attention of followers who are the academic equivalent of celebrity 'friends' on Facebook. This is one of the ways that ResearchGate markets its platform; users are informed that the RG Score can be used to 'leverage standing within the scientific community',[64] which perhaps hints at practices which are analogous to the use of performance-enhancing drugs in sport. We return to that issue shortly, but first we should explain why this type of visibility can be understood not merely as a game, which suggests a degree of playfulness, but as a *serious* and *strategic* game that connects to something Stephen Ball mentions in the quote above – the issue of being judged based on one's performance. To be visible is to be ranked and judged relative to peers and rivals, and this is not necessarily without consequence.

It might be argued that the RG Score is not a credible measure of impact and is not seen as valid on the part of researchers or research institutions. The short answer to that would be 'not yet'. Conventional bibliometrics are already being supplemented by an innovation known as 'altmetrics', which capture impact in the form of mentions in newspapers, on blogs and social-networking platforms such as CiteULike, Mendeley and Twitter ('Twitter demographics' for example log tweeters who 'share an article').[65] Websites for academic journals are also beginning to resemble Academia.edu and ResearchGate. An example is the Taylor & Francis Group, which has added the number of 'views' and 'altmetric score' to articles published in its extensive portfolio of journals, while also adopting a 'What's Trending' approach to marketing its books. Professional standing is becoming a matter of who is following who and how big the numbers are (citations, views, downloads, reads, followers, tweets), and if this helps to enhance one's visibility and reputation, then that, too, can be leveraged by plugging into Google Scholar Metrics, which is marketed by Google as 'an easy way for authors to quickly gauge the visibility and influence of recent articles in scholarly publications'.[66] By harvesting and collating data, Google Scholar Metrics enables researchers to capture the 'impact' of their research and to express this in numerical form. Numbers, then, are a key feature of this serious and strategic game.

Richard Price, founder and CEO of Academia.edu, uses the phrase 'credibility metrics' to describe this game of numbers. In an interview with Price published in *Scientific American*, Hadas Shema notes that publishing in a top-ranked academic journal has long been considered a 'stamp of approval'. Price responds by noting that the 'historical' peer-review process uses the opinions of reviewers as 'a proxy for the opinion of the scientific community'. The future, he says, is 'a family of credibility metrics' that 'reflect the sentiment of the scientific community'.[67] This evaluative shift – from 'opinion' to 'sentiment' – might warrant discussion in its own right, but here we want to focus on credibility metrics in the round. The individual researcher is becoming a self-administered micro-enterprise, or as Price puts it, 'we are moving towards a world where the personal brands of scientists are starting to eclipse those of journals ... The individual is increasingly going to be the person who drives the distribution of their own work and also the work of other people they admire'.[68] It hardly matters whether Price is stating a fact or embracing a normative vision when he says that 'what will drive the adoption of credibility metrics is the competitive spirit in the scientific community'.[69] In a situation where tenure-track jobs are scarce and where academic labour is becoming more precarious, in the words of Price, 'you are incentivised' to find a way to stand out.

We noted earlier that academics do not have to fear the equivalent of anti-doping agencies. However, performance is still wedded to credibility, particularly given the ease with which Google Scholar Metrics, altmetrics and platforms such as Academia.edu can be gamed (or 'leveraged' to borrow from ResearchGate). In an experiment aimed specifically at demonstrating how Google Scholar Metrics can be manipulated, three researchers from the University of Granada and the University of Navarra – Emilio Delgado López-Cózar, Nicolás Robinson-García and Daniel Torres Salinas created six false documents, each citing 129 papers from their own research team. Links to full-text versions of the fabricated documents were uploaded to a webpage under the University of Granada domain. Google Scholar subsequently indexed the documents, and to give an indication of the difference this can make to an individual researcher's profile, Torres Salinas presents two screenshots of his public profile 'before' and 'after the experiment'. His total citations rose from 226 to 415, while his i10-index (which captures articles with at least ten citations) more than doubled, from 7 to 17.[70]

This strategic feature of credibility metrics mirrors Academia.edu's business model, which exploits the credibility of the open-access movement. The basic idea behind the open-access movement is to create a type of commons whereby knowledge is freely accessible to all as opposed to being a commodity which is privately owned and traded on the market. Academia.edu certainly makes research freely available, but that is about as close at it comes to the open-access ideal, because this is a commercial platform designed to mine data. As of 18 October 2015, more than twenty-six million academics had signed up to Academia.edu and posted seven million papers, which are available for download.[71] The platform enables users to send messages to each other, to comment on draft research papers, and to view their personal analytics on a dashboard that logs profile views and document views. This flow of data *is* the business model, and Academia.edu is arguably way ahead of competitors, such as the Taylor & Francis Group, when it comes to leveraging trends in research. As Richard Price explains:

> The goal is to provide trending research data to R&D [research and development] institutions that can improve the quality of their decisions by 10–20 per cent. The kind of algorithm that R&D companies are looking for is a 'trending papers' algorithm, analogous to Twitter's trending topics algorithm. A trending papers algorithm would tell an R&D company which are the most impactful papers in a given research area in the last 24 hours, 7 days, 30 days, or any time period. Historically it's been very difficult to get this kind of data ... As scientific activity is moving online, it's becoming easier to track which papers are getting more attention from the top scientists.[72]

Academia.edu taps into the open-access ideal, thereby aligning its business model with the positive meanings associated with transparency. Yet what Price is describing shades into open-source intelligence (OSINT). OSINT is a form of surveillance that harvests, analyses and repurposes information which is in 'plain sight' – basically the same method used to generate altmetrics.[73] The growing popularity of social media has augmented the possibilities of OSINT and algorithmic data-surveillance because, unlike phone calls and emails, much of the information posted on platforms such as Facebook, Twitter and Academia.edu is publicly accessible.

One issue that arises at the intersection of OSINT and altmetrics relates to the use of data harvested from open-source networks. This may be repurposed without our knowledge or consent, the upshot being that we may be unwittingly or inadvertently recruited into practices and processes that we deem ethically questionable or politically unacceptable. Media theorist Gary Hall makes an important observation concerning this complex relationship between the open-access ideal, Academia. edu's business model, and the field of higher education, which folds back onto Williams' framing of academic freedom as a marketplace. Although academic research is increasingly reliant on private funding, the majority of academics are employed in publicly funded institutions, and Hall is surely correct when he argues that Academia. edu has a 'parasitical relationship to the public education system ... academics are labouring for it for free to help build its privately-owned for-profit platform by providing the aggregated input, data and attention value'.[74]

Whether one games the system or plays true, the game itself is comparable to competition in the sporting arena, that is, freedom as a glass cage. As with the nineteenth-century classroom, power is exercised in the form of a gaze that keeps a watchful eye over one and all, except that now the gaze is also decentralised and reversed, with those who are watched also competing to be seen. The French philosopher and social theorist Michel Foucault gave a name to this fusion of power and visibility: he called it 'the eye of power'.[75] To come back to the notion of disadvantage as a way of framing inequality, the glass cage is an instrument in a contest whereby visibility becomes a way of catching up, keeping up and getting ahead. By constructing our own personal glass cages, we freely participate in a competition driven by the logic of ranking and rivalry, a contest that distinguishes the best from the rest – and this reinforces the ethos of enterprise and innovation in at least two ways: we ensnare ourselves in a business model fuelled by algorithmic surveillance, and we generate numbers that allow our digital-doubles to be compared and ranked, which in turn feeds back into the ranking of academic labour within the institutional setting.

The glass cage accelerates the transformation of academia into a competitive arena that is configured as a race without a finishing line. This is not simply a race among winners and losers, it is also a race to remain in the race, to not fall too far behind (which is to be judged deficient and thus a liability rather than an asset to the organisation). Moreover, this is a field of power relations that extends from the macro-political level of state policy and international trends in higher education, through the institutional level of managed and measured performance, to the micro-politics of peer relations and self-administered glass cages. In short, this is much more than a mode of control whereby visible power is exercised by managers over line-workers (or anti-doping agencies over athletes). In fact, it is a highly decentred network of relations shaped also by intangible and invisible forms of power. Through a blend of pressures and constraints – some more visible than others – and also through a spectrum of inducements that reward participation in zero-sum contests that distinguish winners from losers, freedom is being scripted in ways that foreclose on other possible ways of practising freedom. So how might we begin to edit or rewrite the script?

In concluding this section we outline an initial approach to this question by using the lens of art. We continue this line of discussion in the next section, so it is important to stress (as mentioned in the introduction) that we are not attributing some sort of special transformative power to art or to artists. To mention briefly the sporting arena again, it is simply a truism that many sports are competitions that fuel emotionally charged highs and lows, not merely for the players or contestants, but also for fans and spectators; these highs and lows map onto the experience of winning and losing. Yet even in the realm of sport, competition need not be an obsessive quest to win at all costs. There is a faint – barely noticeable, yet emergent – idea in the sport of cycling at the moment, expressed by those who are disenchanted with the widespread obsession with optimising performance at the cost of deriving pleasure from racing a bicycle. Some racers now switch off their computerised hardware (devices fitted to bicycles that provide real-time data such as the rider's power output and heart rate), choosing instead to ride on 'feel' – bodily sensations that the rider tunes into, aligning these with other sensations, such as the wind on one's face, the joy of moving at speed, the moments of intense concentration and physical effort when the rider feels *alive*.[76] An equivalent example in academia would be the freedom to embark on open-ended and creative approaches to teaching and research, that is, without first having to stipulate what the 'learning outcomes' or the 'impact' will be. This is something we want to consider in the remainder of this section. We also want to devote some discussion to the collaborative nature of creative pursuits and endeavours, because this is overshadowed and to some extent eclipsed by the scripted practice of freedom we have been examining here.

Freedom as a Scripted Practice

Consider the difference between a house painter and an artist who paints. The house painter works to a script, which is the equivalent of an architect's drawing. The script might be produced by an interior designer or the owner of the house to be decorated, but either way the desired end product determines what will be done and how it will be done. Though this is skilled and knowledgeable work, the tradesperson is basically a tool in a managed process. In the case of an artist who paints – and though this is by no means a rule without exception – the artist who knows exactly what she will produce before the process even commences is likely to make the artistic equivalent of a decoration. Creativity is more usually an open-ended undertaking guided by ideas, experience, technique, skill and also individual talent, but to peel away the layers of the finished work would likely reveal a process very different to the scripted labour of a house painter.

A concrete example of what is at stake in this distinction is Pablo Picasso's *Guernica*, a painting that depicts the horrors of war in a highly visceral way and on a monumental scale (the piece is 3.5 metres high and 7.7 metres long). The room that houses *Guernica* in the Museum Sofia in Madrid also exhibits a series of photographs documenting how Picasso reworked his original vision. His initial sketches offer glimpses of what the finished piece would eventually look like, but there is no way of seeing the end in the beginning. In addition, Picasso was not alone with his work. It was his lover, Dora Maar – an artist in her own right it must be added – who used her camera to record the painting's evolution, and her presence must be seen as contributing to the creative process, just as the viewer's presence helps to produce the meaning of the finished painting. Furthermore, there is also the complex relationship between context and artistic process to consider. Against the backdrop of the Spanish Civil War, *Guernica* was commissioned by the Republican government for the Spanish Pavilion at the International Exposition in Paris in 1937, and, in the context of the Exposition, the painting was a cypher in a deadly political game, with the Soviet Union and Nazi Germany using their exhibition spaces to stage an ideological battle for supremacy.[77]

Is there a lesson to be derived from the story of *Guernica*? We think there is, and it is this: creativity is a *social* process that may be captured by political forces. The optimistic theme of the 1937 International Exposition was 'Art and Technology in Modern Life'. Yet the reality of modern life at that time was fast becoming anything but optimistic, with art and technology pressed into the service of industrial warfare and genocide. Today, art, technology and just about everything else becomes raw material to fuel the Enterprise Society, with space for creativity eviscerated even as the myth of genius is sustained. What has become abundantly clear is that there is no essential correspondence between the genius myth and creativity. Instead, the myth of genius is engendering intense rivalry among individuals, transforming the practice of freedom into a race to outdo each other in entirely predictable ways. Consistent with a drop-down menu culture, the measure of success, achievement and excellence is pre-scripted and dangled in front of us like a target that we should aim our efforts at, so that striving to be the best becomes an exercise in competitive conformity. In academia, for example, the game of numbers cultivates a version of the genius myth by attaching a score to individual pieces of work and individual authors, which in turn generates a hierarchy of value. This obscures the extent to which producing research is a diffuse and *relational* process shaped by ideas and insights that circulate in space and travel through time: suddenly something that Aristotle wrote nearly two and a half millennia ago takes on new significance in light of present concerns; a solution to a sticky research problem emerges unexpectedly whilst on a hiking holiday with friends; a PhD student struggling with writer's block experiences a eureka moment while watching a movie; an undergraduate student participating in a seminar sees something new in a text the lecturer has been using for years. All of this intellectual labour exhibits moments of dialogue and collaboration, and creativity thrives in situations where our minds are open to the possibilities of unexpected encounters and unconventional associations. We don't always know what we want to say or write or paint or make until we begin the process of actually *doing* it, and, even then, we may not know what it is that we're trying to create until after we've *done* it. To speak of collaboration in the field of academic research tends to evoke the image of a team of experts working relentlessly towards a singular goal by dividing the overall project into smaller work packages. However, this is but one of the many ways of engaging with others in producing something one could not have produced alone.

To enlarge this insight is to recognise that the practice of freedom is itself a collaborative undertaking. As the interweaving of multiple cultural practices – which have come into existence gradually through the lacing together of visible, intangible and invisible power – freedom is not merely scripted but also *pre*-scripted (historically constituted) and *pre-scriptive* (sanctions may apply when deviating from the script). In the context of the Enterprise Society and in contrast to open-ended creativity, the freedom to be innovative and enterprising fuels a machine that – though powered by human effort, talent, initiative, skill and imagination – disciplines these distinctly human 'inputs' through accountancy practices that divide 'outputs' that count from others that count for very little. When peoples' jobs, security and futures are on the line, and when outputs must have 'impact' in order to count, then it is inevitable that the machine will begin to condition what is done and how it is done. In short, the game of innovation and enterprise constrains the freedom to engage in creative endeavour. However, this is by no means the entire picture, and the field of collaborative and socially engaged art is an important part of the larger story, though given what has been discussed above, we need to stress the difference between collaborative/engaged art and works such as *Guernica*. Art that resides solely within the realm of aesthetics is too easily rendered harmless by market forces or else hijacked and held hostage for political ends. Instead, we are referring to practices that purposefully cross the boundary between collaborative art and different forms of activism; practices located at the threshold of politics and aesthetics; practices that generate spaces where alternative social forms can emerge, and where unscripted futures can be imagined. Importantly, such imagined futures need not be framed as final destinations. As provisional horizons they can remain open to chance encounters, unforeseen antagonisms and unplanned deviations, thereby generating new directions and new horizons. But perhaps the real urgency of imagining alternative futures is that this can provide critical vantage points from which to view the here and now. It is to this task that we now turn by adopting a dialogical mode of presentation.

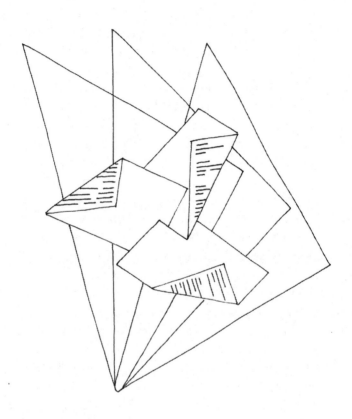

Reimagining the Practice of Freedom

In the previous sections we focused on how the practice of freedom is shaped by visible, intangible and invisible power. We also tried to show how the power/freedom nexus is historically constituted, so that history 'lives' in how we think, speak and act, and this in turn – at least to some extent – conditions what we envision as we look towards the future. What we have covered so far might be distilled into the somewhat obvious point that power constrains the scope of freedom, but it is arguably important to understand the *how* of this. What we have yet to consider, as mentioned in the introduction, is how power can also alter the degrees of freedom available to us in the context of the Enterprise Society. To engage with this question necessitates a shift in the framing of freedom, moving from the pervasive emphasis on freedom as embodied in individuals, to freedom that emerges through concerted action.[78] Making this move is also to turn away from an individualised understanding of equality which is, as discussed earlier, tied to the notion of disadvantage. In the context of the Enterprise Society, this translates into the opportunity to participate in a race to nowhere, an endless striving to catch up, to keep up and to get ahead. In short, freedom in the Enterprise Society engenders an equality of inequality.[79]

Our starting point for this section is that the power/freedom nexus as currently configured is contingent and contestable. There are other ways of enacting the relationship between power and freedom, and herein lies the possibility of generating a very different type of equality; not an equality of inequality vis-à-vis the discourse of disadvantage, but something else, something *other*. What that *other* might be is not for us to determine. It is our contention that whatever alternatives might arise through concerted action must come from practice itself, which is the focus of discussion in this section. Moreover, our discussion is by no means restricted to the exchange of personal ideas and viewpoints. Instead, we focus our discussion on Fiona's collaborative practice, which spans approximately twelve years and multiple projects.

We thought it would be useful, particularly for readers unfamiliar with this body of work, to open this section with an overview of Fiona's practice. We would also like to make a suggestion as to how to read these final two sections, which are essentially layers of the same constellation of thought, practice and experience. As noted earlier, in the final section of this book we present extracts from a public performance called *Natural History of Hope*. What we would like to suggest is for readers to go to Section 4 now, to read the extracts from *Natural History of Hope* before reading the rest of this section, and then to read the extracts again later. We think this slightly unconventional way of reading, which is generally discouraged for reasons captured by the phrase 'spoiler alert', will enrich the reader's understanding of our dialogue below.

In poetry the word *caesura* is sometimes used to describe a 'cut' or pause in a verse or text. We will use this word to mark a space here, so that the extracts from *Natural History of Hope* can both foreground and follow the remainder of this section.

Caesura...

Fiona: As indicated above, I'll open this dialogue with an overview of my practice, and it's important to note that the international field of collaborative and socially engaged art represents a hugely diverse and disparate set of practices, with multiple genealogies traceable through the history of art, theatre, social movements, activism as well as community development and education practice.[80] While socially engaged arts practitioners are all generally interested in real-life political change, contemporary practice is characterised by diversity rather than uniformity, with a wide-ranging spectrum of intentions and approaches crucial to keeping the field alive and in tension with itself. I would characterise my practice as place-based, collaborative, durational and multi-faceted, always working across sector, discipline and knowledge with a range of co-creators.

Since my arrival in Rialto (Dublin) in 2004 as an artist in residence,[81] I have built my practice alongside a well-established community organisation – Rialto Youth Project (RYP). Our collaborative practice as artist and organisation has involved an open-ended and multi-layered engagement with complex themes such as *power* and *hope*. Engaging diverse individuals and groups in long-term relational enquiries, the practice promotes collective processes, working across disciplines and fields of knowledge. To borrow a phrase from artist Jay Koh, my practice could be described as 'relationally responsive', not bound by the limits of a facilitator's role, but not entirely autonomous either.[82] The learning and public outputs in our practice are not prescribed, but instead are to be found by those who come together to collaborate over time.

The initial years were focused on positioning my practice alongside a team of youth workers and developing an approach to collaboration based on our shared interests while also holding on to our differences, after which we established a collective called What's the Story? (2007–11).[83] With the aim of pushing the boundaries of collaboration between young people, youth workers and artist, the collective's practice became focused on

Figure 1: *Anonymous; Reading, Narrative & Memory,* by What's the Story? Collective, Rialto, 2008. Video stills by Enda O'Brien. Collaged by Fiona Whelan. © Fiona Whelan and Rialto Youth Project.

an intense exploration of power, both in the collaborative working relationship of the group itself, and in our individual lived experiences. Central to the process was a collection of personal anonymous stories, gathered over time from members of the collective and other young people attending RYP, exploring moments in individuals' lives where feelings of power and powerlessness were experienced. Over two further years, the gathered stories moved from private to public, in a series of events staged in community spaces and contemporary art venues. This included two participatory reading events (Figures 1 & 2), two films, a mobile cinema which travelled nationally and internationally, and a major exhibition and residency in The LAB Gallery in Dublin.

This accumulation of events constituted a reflexive process whereby diverse stories were reworked and presented in increasingly public environments, encountering various publics who were targeted and invited to listen and engage. What started as recollections of personal experiences of power and powerlessness became key points of exploration into state power, in particular policing, a theme that ran through many of the gathered stories.

Figure 2: *The Day in Question*, by What's the Story? Collective, Irish Museum of Modern Art, Dublin, 2009. Video still by Enda O'Brien © Fiona Whelan and Rialto Youth Project.

In the spirit of the dialogical approach that the collective had been developing, engaging directly with An Garda Síochána (the Irish police force) became an important feature of the project. During the participatory reading event, *The Day in Question* (2009, Figure 2), a newly recruited group of gardaí (police officers) read aloud a collection of young people's anonymous testimonies in the presence of the collective and a group of invited witnesses. These testimonies included diverse and largely negative experiences of policing – in homes, in garda stations and in public space – as well as a selection of other stories reflecting community life and individual dreams, presenting a nuanced and complex existence.

A year later, the project climaxed with *Policing Dialogues* (Figures 3 and 4), which included an exhibition and a residency in The LAB Gallery in Dublin, bringing together young people, youth workers, educators,

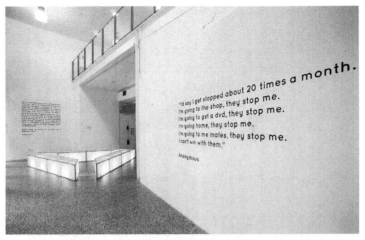

Figure 3: *Policing Dialogues*, by What's the Story? Collective, The LAB, Dublin, 2010. Photograph by Michael Durand. © Dublin City Council Arts Office.

Figure 4: *Policing Dialogues*, by What's the Story? Collective, The LAB, Dublin, 2010. © Fiona Whelan.

academics and members of An Garda Síochána in an active exploratory space. Young people's stories of policing from across the city continued to accumulate over the duration of the residency, which fed a further set of live encounters between young people and police. The gallery was closed to the public for two days, facilitating dialogue between the collective and the same group of gardaí, which highlighted hierarchical structures of power and embedded cultural practices in both the gardaí and community, as well as gaps in garda training that contributed to some gardaí feeling ill-equipped to police areas of Dublin. An inquiry into garda training also ran for the duration of the residency, committed to exploring how best to incorporate awareness of power, dignity and respect into relationships between gardaí and young people, leading to the co-development of new local training for future gardaí assigned to our policing district.[84]

In 2012, core features of the practice developed during What's the Story? were taken and fed into the *Natural History of Hope* (2012–16) project, not as a formula, but as a set of transferable principles inherent in the approach developed between artist and community organisations. This brought another diverse group of people together, again committed to a long-term process, but this time exploring contemporary equality issues in women's lives across generations.[85] Over three years, local performative events were staged with an emphasis on listening, meals were organised where relationships were forged, and multiple workshops took place where ideas were born. The development of a temporary local school built around values of exploring power, sharing personal truth and acting in solidarity became a key phase of work. As a feature of a short-term residency in Studio 468 (2016),[86] we reconstructed the studio space as a school for women of different generations, reframing our collective approach and the methods we had used in the process as a new form of gender-based pedagogy, which operated without designated teachers and without a curriculum, instead using the three core principles identified above. Although formalising our approach as a form of pedagogy was occasionally counter productive, the repositioning of our practice into this new context and pedagogical framing stimulated a collective of women to imagine a highly public moment where the stories could take form differently.

While the previous project had quickly identified policing – a very visible form of power – as a strong theme to pursue, *Natural History of Hope* unveiled multiple overlapping realities of class and gender inequality, highlighting layers of invisible and intangible power. As a result, the public performance of *Natural History of Hope* in the Project Arts Centre, Dublin (2016, see figures 5, 8, 9 and 10) involved a cast of thirty women representing this complexity.[87] Using lived experience coupled with external analyses from a range of professionals who were invited to engage with the stories over the duration of the project, the cast would speak back to multiple oppressive forces.[88] Themes of class, death, the liability of men,[89] gendered identity, lack of safe space, struggle

Figure 5: *Natural History of Hope*, by Fiona Whelan, Rialto Youth Project and Brokentalkers, Project Arts Centre, Dublin, 2016. © Ray Hegarty.

for dignity and the affective domain were identified and inter-woven into a landscape in which the female protagonist, a mannequin called Hope (Figure 5), would attempt to survive and if possible to thrive. Complex social themes could not be simplified here as they crashed against each other at different stages of the mannequin's life, the cast positioned as powerful women, yearning for something better for Hope. Taking the work out of its geographical site of origin has always been a feature of the practice, bringing the material and collective authors into spaces of conversation with layered sets of power relations. Presenting this work in a contemporary art venue during the centenary of the 1916 Rising,[90] and in light of the Waking the Feminists campaign,[91] created other lenses for the work and highlighted key questions around the power and representation of gendered work-ing-class experience.[92]

While *power* and *hope* are overarching themes that frame the two projects respectively, and while multiple sub-themes emerged and overlapped within the pro-cesses and public works, I'm increasingly interested in putting the practice into conversation with discours-es and practices concerned with *freedom*. As outlined in the introduction to this book, we can distinguish between freedom *from*, freedom *to* and freedom *as,* which becomes helpful when trying to make sense of complex social structures that effect the order of things, but what might be most beneficial here is to return to the blur-rier terrain surrounding the practice and imagination of freedom that can be elicited in art projects such as these. Holding on to complexity is something that we have insisted on in both projects, striving to create com-plex polyvocal encounters and avoiding any reduction of these themes to engender simple interpretations or sin-gular solutions. Perhaps I can begin by asking you about this somewhat fraught relationship between power and freedom, particularly given the current political climate.

Kevin: I agree that the macro-political context offers a line of approach to the micro-politics of your practice, but in turn your collaborative practice puts the broad-er context in perspective. What we're seeing now is not necessarily an historical rupture or political tsunami as many commentators have suggested, but rather some-thing that seems to be deeply rooted in the issues we've framed by using the idea of the Enterprise Society. I'll try to substantiate this point if I may. In years to come, 2016 is likely to be remembered as the year that demagogues appropriated the ideal of freedom, using it to construct stories of hatred and resentment that reduce complex realities to simplistic fictions that fan the flames of racism and xenophobic nationalism. Marine Le Pen from the French Front National, for example, responded to Donald Trump's election as 'the victory of freedom', echoing not only the sentiment but also the words used by Brexiters during the build-up to the referendum in Britain.[93] There has been a lot of speculation as to how to explain the unexpected groundswell of popular support for Trump and Brexit, and without claiming to have an answer to this question, it does seem to be the case that demagoguery succeeded in leveraging fears and insecurities which are very real in the context of the Enterprise Society – that is, the extent to which life is becoming increasingly precarious for so many people. In Ireland we've seen a version of this politics of fear following the bank bailout in 2008, and it was very much to the fore during the last general election (February 2016) when the outgoing government attempted to blackmail the electorate by insisting that what was at stake was a choice between stability – meaning more austerity – and chaos. But what exactly does 'stability' mean, particularly to people at the margins of whatever it is that the Enterprise Society has to offer? And if stability means more of the same, then what kind of future awaits people framed by policy discourse as 'disadvantaged'?

Through your practice with RYP, you've been engaging with these sorts of questions for more than a decade – long before Trump and Brexit appeared on the radar of political discourse – through a series of projects that span the transition from 'Celtic Tiger' economy to the catastrophe of 'Ireland Inc.'. One long-term project (What's the Story?), was anchored in stories of power, while more recently (*Natural History of Hope*) the focus of the work seems to have shifted somewhat, so that although the practice is still informed by stories of power, the public manifestation of the work might be framed as the power of story. Something I need to stress here is the importance of distinguishing stories that promote racism and division (Trump and Brexit) from the forms of storytelling at the core of your practice, which engender a process of mutual learning and possibly also shared understanding. So, to take stock: stories of power and the power of stories, and together these span visible, intangible and invisible power. These are among the co-ordinates of your practice, which is anchored in the field of art and yet is also much more than art. Maybe we can use these coordinates to engage with your practice, beginning with your own story?

You studied as an art student at a sort of pivotal moment, that is, when new academic programmes tailored to socially engaged art were getting underway in at least some art colleges on the island of Ireland. This is quite a recent development, and art education still tends to be geared towards what the writer, curator and arts administrator Declan McGonagle refers to as 'signature practice'.[94] By unplugging art from its social context and material conditions of existence, signature practice cultivates and sustains what was presented above in the context of academia as the genius myth. In contrast to the pervasiveness of signature practice, you've forged a very distinctive pathway by developing a collaborative practice that engages with people and place. To what extent was it a conscious decision to work in this way, I mean, was there an element of serendipity to it – like a door opening that you may or may not have walked through?

Fiona: It's hard to know when my journey to becoming a collaborative, socially-engaged artist began. I don't recall much exposure in my primary art degree in the Nineties to anything other than signature practice. On the contrary, I recall the competitive nature of the art world, highlighted in our final year when it was stated that 'in ten years, two of you will be artists'. This was not shared so the remaining group might consider how they could apply art thinking to other pursuits, but rather to communicate our impending failure and to drive us to work harder in competition with each other. I recall the first opportunity we were given to enter such a race (outside of the obvious hierarchical grading structure), when we had to choose to put our names forward for a graduate prize, a studio award which would be issued to two remarkable graduating students. I didn't apply. I would have liked the studio. I loved making work and had only just found an approach to making paintings that was really exciting me, but as a twenty-one-year-old,

I felt deeply afraid and turned off by the singular and competitive nature of the world that was being offered. As I finished my degree I had become a product of the dominant educational tradition supporting signature practice. Motivated by issues of inequality, it took a few years for me to reposition myself and regenerate an art practice as I went on to engage in two new post-graduate courses that were literally emerging in tandem with my needs, becoming part of a first generation of professionalised practitioners in Ireland in the field of community-based and public art practice.[95] But equally important in my educational story is the timing of my arrival in RYP as an artist in residence.

As you highlighted in a previous collaboration of ours, the language of power was radically altered during the 1980s and 1990s, both in Ireland and the EC/EU.[96] We spoke about the effect this had on the community arts movement, which had started out as a deeply political set of practices motivated by issues of inequality and the pursuit of 'cultural democracy', reframed over time and through state involvement, using the language of 'disad-vantage' and social 'exclusion'. Importantly during this time, while youth work was being steered by policies with minimal focus on inequality, some organisations, includ-ing RYP, refused to endorse the depoliticised language in the state's classification of Rialto as 'disadvantaged'. Instead, RYP adopted the defiant language of 'oppres-sion' and 'marginalisation', while building a strong capaci-ty for arts-based work committed to the exploration and representation of social issues.[97] Arriving in 2004, I was early enough in my career to allow the years that would follow to be truly formative. My engagement with RYP created a dialogue between strong community development and youth-work values coupled with legacies of community arts that existed in Rialto and contemporary critical discourses occupying the field of collaborative and socially engaged practice that preoccupied me, creating a period of learning and unlearning for me.

The symbol of the triangle that has run throughout my work emerged after a number of years immersed in this context. It began as a response to the triangulation of subject positions that occupied the field, that of the artist, the professional attached to community organisation, and the user of the organisation who is often classified in some way by their attachment to it (such as 'client' or 'service user'). This configuration of relationships is typically hierarchical, with the artist and organisation's staff member developing structures that participants, in this case youth, would be invited to avail of. Our triangle was intended to be laid flat and to be non-hierarchical from the outset – a collective space from within which all decisions would be made. However, if in doing this we had also removed our subject identities, we would have risked suggesting some kind of neutralised equality that would mask the cultural hierarchy we were working to overcome, or what I've described elsewhere as a dangerous move towards a model of social 'inclusion'.[98] A commitment to equality became a starting point rather than a destination of the work. Holding and working through the complexi-

Figure 6: *The Day in Question*, by What's the Story? Collective, Irish Museum of Modern Art, Dublin, 2009. Video still by Enda O'Brien. © Fiona Whelan and Rialto Youth Project.

ties attached to each of our points on the triangle was important, leading to many discussions examining our differences in knowledge, class, age and background. I recall a very early conversation in the process where I posed a question to the group asking who had the most power in the room. Following an intense discussion in which my privileged background and my leadership role were named, as well as youth workers' organisational power, young people began to recognise their own power if they acted collectively, succinctly put by one young woman when she pointed out: 'Without us, you wouldn't have a job'.[99] Over time, power relations were explored, confronted and embodied, and we became less preoccupied with our distinct points of the triangle, and recognised the potential of the hybrid collaborative space in the centre of the triangle, which had become both a space of collective power and a space of imagining. New triangles were then constructed whereby subject positions changed, such as during *The Day in Question* when members of the collective sat together on one side of a triangle in dialogue with gardaí, while witnesses were seated on the third side (Figure 6).

Kevin: I'm drawn to how you describe the triangle as a way of flattening power relations that might otherwise exist as hierarchies, because it occurs to me that this might also help to prevent dialogue from becoming polarised. What I mean is that refusing hierarchy in favour of horizontal relationships doesn't in itself address what I'll refer to here as 'the problem of power', meaning power relations that engender inequalities and social suffering. For example, dialogue is often invoked as an alternative to violence when there's a need to resolve conflict between opposing sides or forces in a dispute. In this respect 'dialogue' becomes synonymous with binary divisions, so that contentious issues are framed in terms of right and wrong, good and bad, friends and enemies, and so on. To refer back to your earlier remark about the current political climate, this type of polarising discourse is extremely palpable right at this point in time. In contrast to this, the triangulated process you describe exceeds the grip of binary thinking. If tools are required to engage critically with the problem of power, then the triangle might be described as one such tool, given that it is both a method and a mode of representation. This brings me back to stories of power and the power of story in the context of your practice, which, as you point out, has gradually moved inwards from the edges or sides of the triangle, thereby generating other ways of engaging with the problem of power. Can you say more about this?

Fiona: In the way that the triangle both acknowledges multiple subject positions while offering another space in the centre, presenting multiple personal stories in all the public work is an important feature in the development of polyvocal encounters. During the time of What's the Story? Collective, a collection of sixty anonymous stories detailing lived experiences of power and powerlessness was the bedrock for all the public work. For the subsequent project, *Natural History of Hope*, approximately 250 anonymous stories were gathered from women and girls living and working in Rialto (including myself and the other youth-project staff working on the project), all gathered orally in private, each transcribed and co-edited with the storyteller. These collections of stories then transitioned through a number of encounters and accumulative stages, communicating complex social themes from multiple perspectives. The events have been described previously as forms of agonistic dialogue, which draws on Chantal Mouffe's theory of agonistic democracy, where multiple voices are heard and consensus is not a priority.[100] Related to the more familiar notion of *agonising*, the overarching objective of an agonistic approach to concerted action is to keep the process of contestation alive, so that power relations cannot sediment so deeply in social consciousness that we lose sight of the fact that who we are, what we are, is fundamentally contingent. Working with diverse personal testimonies assists in preventing binary oppositions or a prioritisation of consensus; rather, it encourages the opening up and exploration of complex themes.

Anonymity plays an important role in this dialogical space, first introduced as a device to allow people to explore their experiences safely without feeling disloyal or exposing themselves or others to unnecessary risk (when sharing our lived experiences, we are often inadvertently sharing those of our families and loved ones, too). However, the potential of anonymity grew as it also allowed people to freely engage alongside their anonymous narratives, as part of a collection, while not feeling bound to the particular version they had shared. In many cases storytellers' relationships to their own stories changed as they journeyed from private to public, with anonymity recognised as an important component within the construction of such polyvocal events.

Kevin: In light of recent events on the world political stage and the ways in which images and information circulate within and across media networks, for many people the tactic of anonymity would likely call to mind the subversive interventions of hacktivists operating under the banner of Anonymous,[101] or maybe activists within the Occupy movement. In both cases the Guy Fawkes mask that featured in the Hollywood movie *V for Vendetta* is appropriated, being used to mask the individual's identity while also signifying that the resistant 'I' is, in fact, the collective resistance of 'we the ninety-nine percent'. I wonder, though, whether anonymity is somewhat different in the context of projects such as *The Day in Question*, *Policing Dialogues* and *Natural History of Hope*. As you point out, in all of these projects the

Figure 7: *Policing Dialogues*, by What's the Story? Collective, The LAB, Dublin, 2010. Photograph by Michael Durand. © Dublin City Council Arts Office.

process builds from stories which are unique to individuals, but which subsequently enter into dialogue with other stories by being spoken aloud in public settings, read in the privacy of the purpose-built reading room during The LAB residency (Figure 7), and performed on stage. If I could distil something from your reflection above – that anonymity is part of a process whereby individual/subjective stories are re-enacted as relational experiences within public settings – then this mode of storytelling becomes a way of communicating the problem of power while also enabling people to bear witness to the various forms it takes, such as class inequality, generational power relations, patriarchy, and so on. However, viewed as part of the larger cultural context, this mode of anonymity also seems to operate on another level as well.

The ancient root of the word anonymous translates as 'without name' or 'nameless', and is arguably shadowed by words like 'common' and 'community', as in held in common or shared by all. Perhaps it's merely a few zig-zagging steps to move from 'anonymous' to 'common' to 'public' and back again? More to the point, in the context of your work with RYP, anonymity seems to function as a way of renouncing signature practice, which is not merely a pervasive way of assigning authorship and ownership, but also a way of relinquishing responsibility for inequality. We've touched on signature practice in the field of art, but of course this traverses the broader cultural terrain, too – well beyond academia as discussed earlier – often in the form of brands competing for prestige and market share, and this is by no means unrelated to the problematic framing of inequality as 'disadvantage'. The power of the signature can be seen in how it partitions the 'advantaged' from the 'disadvantaged' in such a way that this division appears apolitical – whether it signifies individuals, small companies or mega-corporations, the signature/brand is associated with qualities that pass for virtue in the Enterprise Society, such as a win-at-all-costs approach to competition, self-promotion, embracing risk and uncertainty as opportunity, and the determination to be a market leader. Yet we need only scratch the surface to see how the signature and the brand operate as a *de*politicised mark of distinction, separating winners from losers and cutting the losers free to fend for themselves, which is how welfare – in the form of conditional entitlements, mandatory work-experience programmes, unpaid internships, and so forth – has been repurposed in the Enterprise Society. In the context of *What's the Story?* and *Natural History of Hope*, you've described how anonymity acts as a way of creating a safe space of communication, but is it also a way of challenging the dominance of signature culture and more besides?

Fiona: You observed in the past that there are two forms of relational power operating simultaneously in the work I do with RYP, one that articulates inequalities between those who exercise power and those who are subject to power, and the other whereby power is co-produced through collaboration.[102] I have described how anonymity has become important when articulating one's own individual experience of inequality, but what's significant in the practice is that individuals who have shared stories anonymously have done so as part of a collective project where their collaborators have engaged in the same process. This can often reposition an individual account of powerlessness, shame or negativity into the space of collaborative power, as structural and systemic power relations are revealed in the collection, and new solidarities built among those involved. Removing authorship of individual accounts also allows the collection of stories to operate with that collaborative power when they are positioned publicly. Anonymity serves to protect the individual authors while simultaneously drawing publics into the substance and complexity of life revealed when the stories are heard as a collection, discouraging any individualising of the material. In each public event, the anonymous nature of the stories contributes to how representation takes place to the individual storytellers, to the collective makers, and to a range of publics concurrently, as part of a continuum of shifting identities that speak back to the depoliticised categorisation of communities considered to be 'disadvantaged'.

In transitioning sets of private individual stories to a shared public realm, we can draw on the German philosopher Hannah Arendt's description of the public realm as a space of shared interest, 'where a plurality of people work to create a world to which they feel they all belong'.[103] The projects were not just about gathering and presenting lived experiences as an act of validation to individuals or communities. These stories were not gathered as part of an external process, not part of formal data, but were part of a creative process in which those who told stories could work alongside their own and others, creating a sense of possibility and a collective imagining of alternatives. As thirty women took to the stage on the first night of *Natural History of Hope* – women living and working in Rialto, together nervous, ready, shoulder to shoulder (Figure 8), intertwined with a script filled with deeply significant personal material,

Figure 8: *Natural History of Hope*, by Fiona Whelan, Rialto Youth Project and Brokentalkers, Project Arts Centre, Dublin, 2016. © Ray Hegarty.

all anonymous and threaded together to be a powerful execution of solidarity and self-representation – it was clear that the two aforementioned forms of relational power (one that articulates inequalities between those who exercise power and those who are subject to power, and the other whereby power is co-produced through collaboration) were converging in the performative moment. The cast were united as women beyond any simplification of roles set out by the field (artist, community worker, participant), bringing their different knowledge and experience together collectively, speaking truth to power.

Figure 9: *Natural History of Hope,* by Fiona Whelan, Rialto Youth Project and Brokentalkers, Project Arts Centre, Dublin, 2016. Programme design by Unthink. © Chris Maguire.

This begins to speak to your question about 'anonymity as a challenge to signature practice' within the field of art, but raises real issues for me, because we opted for different ways of authoring works in the two projects, neither with total satisfaction. In the first instance, the work was all authored by What's the Story? Collective, presented as a horizontal triangle of subject positions: artist, youth workers and young people. While this triangulated platform offered a layer of collective authorship to any individual anonymous account that might be discussed, it raised other issues for the perceived hierarchy of positions when presented in contemporary art spaces, namely the status of me as *the* artist within the collective. The collective framing also reduced the important role of Rialto Youth Project as a key contributor to the project. As *Natural History of Hope* climaxed in a theatre performance, the accompanying printed programme (Figure 9) successfully presented a way of crediting each individual role while leaving all storytellers anonymous for the reasons I've outlined above. The united cast of women, which included me and the RYP staff, didn't distinguish between or highlight any subject positions, which felt like an interesting progression from What's the Story? Similarly, we chose to avoid singular titles of 'Writer' or 'Director', instead acknowledging that the combined practices of a number of collaborators shaped all aspects of the overall performance. However, the overall authoring 'by Fiona Whelan, Rialto Youth Project and Brokentalkers' still felt a little traditional in its signature, not an individual signature but nonetheless a collection of powerful authors – an artist, a youth organisation and a theatre company.

Kevin: The struggle you describe – contesting the grip of signature practice even as you unwillingly end up reproducing it, albeit in modified form – seems to be crucially important to the central question we're exploring in this book, that is, reimagining the practice of freedom. That the collaborations you refer to only partially resolved what I described earlier as the problem of power should perhaps come as no surprise (can we ever resolve these problems once and for all?), but what really matters – to return to something I've touched on already – is that the process generated a method that engages not only with visible power (such as policing) but also with intangible and invisible forms of power. I would see this as an ongoing process that never reaches a final destination, which connects to the concept of agonism as you described it earlier. To link this back to your practice, you mention the 'interesting progression' from the triangular representation of power relations and subject positions to the tensioning of authorship and anonymity in *Natural History of Hope*, and it seems that this progression also generated a different visual vocabulary of power, that is, the use of objects and metaphors to give representational form to power. Will you talk me through this visual vocabulary?

Fiona: The visual symbol of the triangle was central to framing the earlier work exploring power and policing, but what was significant in the *Natural History of Hope* performance was the use of specific metaphors to describe the lived reality to face the character Hope. These metaphors emerged directly from the anonymous transcripts as a lexicon for engaging with social themes among those involved, and so were translated into the performance. Although each metaphor can be seen to represent a core social theme, they each intersect in the performance to represent their complex coexistence.

For example, the bubble referred to in the excerpts of the performance script (Section 4 below) signifies the theme of class, while the liability of men is represented by a shadow, and patriarchy by a wolf. It's been interesting to observe these metaphors emerge from individual stories to unfold in a collective performance on stage, subsequently finding their way back into the site from which they came, with a new power. One performer recently described the moment during the performance when she realised that she has always loved the wolf, how strange it was to be near him on the stage, and how she can now identify him in many situations in her daily life. Another spoke of her current struggle to get out of the bubble and how she had spoken to others around her who felt trapped in it, too. Another spoke of the shadow that silently follows her. The overarching metaphor of the script is of central importance, the performance script becoming a representation of the social script that so many women felt is written for them. This comes to a head towards the end of the performance as Hope lies dying in a chair, her coffin is brought onto the stage, and the script says that she will die. This moment speaks to the opening lines of the performance as we took to the stage, some women recalling a play they had been in twenty years previously:

A lot of the cast from that play are dead now.
They weren't even old when they died.
They learned their lines, they came to rehearsals, and
  they were great in the play, and the audience loved them.

They were full of life, they were talented, they were funny and articulate.
And yet still, they died.
We know that everyone dies.
We're not stupid. We've known that since we were kids.
We know it's natural.
But the amount of them from our play that died.
That's not natural.
It's not right.

Having started our performance with each cast member lighting a candle in memory of those from the previous Rialto performance who didn't make it, the *Natural History of Hope* cast enacted a collective decision to rip up the script, stating that 'Hope's not dying today'. This underscores the extent to which the relationship between power and hope has featured in both projects, and while freedom is implicit in much of what is being explored and clearly hindered by many of the metaphors presented, it's not something we have spoken about much when making the work. Interesting for me was your immediate response having seen the performance, where you described the cast's final act in ripping up the script as a 'bid for freedom', albeit for a mannequin. Could you say more about that in light of what we outlined in the introduction as a drop-down menu of pre-scripted choices in life?

Kevin: What I saw from my place among the audience was a group of women making a joint decision to free themselves from the authority of the script and, by literally *willing* Hope back to life, engaging in a type of creative destruction by erasing the continuity of their own stories, thereby laying claim to a future which is yet to be written. It also occurred to me that the distance between performance and audience sort of collapsed within the compass of that moment. As I watched the women tear up the script on stage, the cast suddenly became their own audience – witnesses to their own actions. Importantly, and this can't be stressed strongly enough in the context of the Enterprise Society, the bid for freedom enacted in *Natural History of Hope* is not necessarily fully formed or fully articulated – it's more like a gesture that opens out a space for freedom to emerge. At the same time, it's very clearly *not* the dominant neoliberal understanding of freedom; it's not about the individual who acquires freedom by participating in zero-sum contests for prestige and rewards, and it's not about individuals expressing their preferences by choosing from a drop-down menu of prescribed choices either. It's something else entirely. You've mentioned the work of Hannah Arendt, and the bid for freedom enacted in *Natural History of Hope* reminds me of how she conceptualises public space, or the commons, as a 'space of appearances'; we appear before each other through our words and actions, and we are thus vulnerable to each other's judgements, but more importantly, when we speak and act in the presence of others, we can – though this very much depends on *how* we relate to each other – grant freedom *to* each other and derive freedom *from* each other.[104]

This is what I saw in that radical gesture, whereby a group of women combined their agency by collectively refusing to live a pre-scripted (as in prescribed) life. By affirming for each other that they could co-author their own story, they were granting freedom to each other while also deriving freedom from each other. This way of practising freedom has become like an endangered species in the Enterprise Society. Let me try to distil these thoughts into a question: would the cast of *Natural History of Hope* have discarded *their own personal* stories in this way, or was that possible only when personal stories became *our* story?

Fiona: So many of the stories gathered together in *Natural History of Hope* described interpersonal relationships that were framed by patriarchy. In the context of such invisible and intangible power, the challenge in moving towards the performance became how to speak to such complex and overlapping power structures. Where the police could literally be invited to sit in the room, the insidious nature of the forms of power described in *Natural History of Hope* were not so easy to speak to or be invited to listen to. The act of resistance in the face of the script being written for Hope was an important gesture. For me, the determination in this action is comparable to the maternal tendency that is witnessed when so many women, many of them quite young, suspend their own ambitions and divert their attention to their children's futures. A steely kind of determination can be observed when women speak of their hopes for their children, an

Figure 10: *Natural History of Hope*, by Fiona Whelan, Rialto Youth Project and Brokentalkers, Project Arts Centre, Dublin, 2016. Video still by Paddy Cahill. © Shoot to Kill.

intolerance of inequality, and a distinct willingness to fight, which is not always present when considering one's own future direction and reality. So I think you are right, the collective act of rewriting the future for Hope seemed more achievable in that moment, than any one individual considering redirecting their own journey against the array of oppressive forces represented.

Kevin: For me and doubtless others like me, by which I mean people who come to *Natural History of Hope* with at least some prior knowledge of collaborations that you've been involved in with other people living and working in the same part of Dublin – among them the young men who told their stories in projects such as *Policing Dialogues*, and who inhabit *Natural History of Hope* as part of the background context – there's something like a narrative quality to the body of work we've been discussing, as though the series of projects are chapters in a much larger story. What I'm trying to say is that my experience of the work – not the individual projects taken in isolation, but the body of work as a whole – is like bearing witness to how patriarchal power intersects with class inequalities, while at the same time class intersects with generational power relations, which in turn intersect with patriarchy, and so on. Of all the metaphors used in *Natural History of Hope*, it's the bubble that stands out to me as giving representational form to this interlacing of power relations (Figure 10).

Fiona: Yes, the bubble is a very strong metaphor that emerged from conversations with many women who used many similar metaphors to describe the reality and effect of living with forms of invisible power such as class. The bubble came to encompass the paradox that was described, feeling like both a sanctuary and a trap; on the one hand a secure place of familiarity, on the other a glue that was holding people down. It was important that in presenting the bubble on stage, it would not be misread as a specific place but rather communicate a barely visible but highly significant layer of power that held a complex existence in people's lives. Importantly, it is a structure which you can look out from but also be observed through, its existence supported by the actions of those on both sides.

Kevin: In the way you've just described the bubble, it seems to be loosely analogous to the metaphor of the glass cage as discussed earlier in the fields of sport and academia – a type of visibility which is also a mirror.

As you point out, to be inside the bubble (and I think this applies also to the glass cage) is to be aware of being visible to those on the 'outside', but there is also the issue of seeing oneself *through* this incoming gaze so that it becomes a mirror. In the case of the glass cage, this is of course the whole point, because the self as presented for public consumption is staged and scripted precisely for that purpose. In the case of the bubble, there is an important difference in that the external gaze is fabricated from concepts such as 'disadvantage', thereby becoming a filter for politics, social science, journalism, and the many other ways in which inequality is mediated and represented so that it becomes 'common sense'. This may elicit sympathy or disdain, but either way it becomes a mode of judgement that diminishes those so perceived. In addition, and this is arguably the most important thing to note in this comparison, the bubble and the glass cage cannot be adequately understood if we focus solely on the repressive features of visible power. These are paradoxical spaces, like your triangle, because they are more than the play of opposites (such as power/resistance or oppression/emancipation): both are enclosures that we ourselves help to sustain through the routine ways in which we practise freedom. Ultimately, for me, the bubble and the glass cage serve as reminders that life is always – to a greater or lesser extent – scripted. To *know* that, not in the superficial sense of knowledge acquired from a book, but as an embodied and visceral *knowing*, is to come face to face with a difficult realisation: the weave of power relations that shapes who we are and provides us with agency also constrains what we might yet become, and this complex weave can never really be fully externalised by attributing it to some symbol of repression such as 'the state' or 'the system' or, indeed, the Enterprise Society. (I'm not suggesting that this is what What's the Story? or *Natural History of Hope* attempt to do, merely that this is how power is often framed by movements struggling for justice and equality.) I think this is a fundamental step towards being the author of one's own story, but, again, the bubble is a reminder that we can't succeed alone – that we always exist in multifaceted relationships with others – and thus authoring one's own story is a collaborative undertaking.

If I could focus specifically on *Natural History of Hope* for a moment, I wonder whether this might be encapsulated by the idea of 'prefiguration', which is a concept used by analysts interested in social-movement culture.[105] This may seem like one of those abstractions used by theorists and philosophers, so let me quickly demystify it. The word is simply derived from 'prefigure' (to foreshadow or imagine beforehand), so essentially this is about heralding or anticipating the change that one would like to see by *enacting* it, thereby bringing the (desired) future into the present. So, in contrast to action that takes the form of means–end rationality (that is, we struggle here and now in order to achieve a predefined goal that exists somewhere in the future), prefiguration brings the future *into* the present by creating new social forms, so that means and ends, struggle and goal, are blended together through *doing*. This way of thinking about concerted action seems to speak to *Natural History of Hope* – not just the performance but the much longer period of time spent working together collectively. Earlier you sketched an outline of this process, you mentioned local performative events that emphasised listening, how meals became a way of building interpersonal relationships, while the establishment of a temporary school afforded a way of exploring power and working in solidarity. Given our discussion on schools and education in Section 1, it is worth noting the very distinct ethos of this temporary school, which wasn't structured by designated roles (teachers and students) that authorise asymmetrical power relations, or bounded by a scripted curriculum. All of this exemplifies prefiguration, which takes me back to that moment on stage where the script is discarded. Might this moment be described as both a fold and a cut? On one level it folds the end of the performance back into the prefigurative process that made the performance possible, so the 'end' of the story is in fact a new beginning. What I mean is that if we understand the self as the embodiment of visible, intangible and invisible power, then the group of women – you among them – who tore up the script at the end of the performance are surely not *the same* people who conceived this project? Four years is a long time in which to shape and be shaped by experiences, relationships, memories and imagined possibilities. It's unlikely that anyone would come out of such a process unchanged. As a 'cut', it hands the story over to the audience, perhaps as an invitation to take responsibility for the future. In fact, this might be a thread that can be traced back through the performance to the very beginning of your collaborations with RYP. In all of the projects we've been discussing, the public staging of anonymous stories makes real (as in, experienced on a deeply visceral level) the ways in which the practice of freedom – what we do *with* each other and what we do *to* each other – can, often without intention, engender a deeply human tragedy which simply cannot be remedied unless we begin to find ways to listen to and learn from each other. Though configured in different ways, the triangle in *The Day in Question* and *Policing Dialogues* and the stage in *Natural History of Hope* are in some sense the same: a way of fielding dialogue, and also – as you pointed out earlier – a way of creating hybrid spaces of learning through listening, learning through doing, learning through witnessing. I'd like to hand these reflections back to you as a final question situated right now, at this precise moment in time: where do you go from here, what comes next?

Fiona: I described earlier how What's the Story? Collective made a commitment to equality as a starting point rather than a destination of the work, which relates to how you position *Natural History of Hope* to a process of prefiguration. Structural change takes time and so I believe it becomes important to practise the desired future from the outset, each stage of work part of an accumulative process. You might recall the first line of *Natural History of Hope* when we take to the stage (Figure 8) and – as noted above – a cast member recalls a play that was performed some years before, explaining that 'a lot of the cast from that play are dead now', one of whom appears on film projected onto the wall behind us. You described earlier how my various projects can be seen as chapters in a larger story. In choosing this beginning to the performance, the cast and script of *Natural History of Hope* created a link to the past and publicly positioned the project as a chapter in a much longer history of creative practice in RYP and part of a continuum of social change. To tail-end the performance with a commitment to keeping Hope alive speaks to new possibilities, but, of course, as the future isn't actually written, the audience is left to decide what might happen next. During the post-show discussion, which took place after the second of three performances between the audience and members of the cast and creative team, an audience member made reference to the cycle of oppression that spirals back through *Natural History of Hope* to the performance from twenty years ago. Calling for significant social change, she expressed her hope that there would not be the need for another such performance in another two decades, where another group continues to fight for a new script.

What's important for the community is that beyond any specific project iteration or artist's engagement, RYP remains a constant presence in the face of oppression and presents a porous skin where the arts flow in and out, calling attention and rupturing norms at particular moments. In a similar vein to the local garda training that we developed during *Policing Dialogues*, I always imagined that beyond the *Natural History of Hope* performances, we would use the material from the project to develop an educational resource for young women and young men related to gender inequality that could be tested in RYP and have further educational value beyond this context. A core group of us are currently working on developing this resource pack, much of which is centred around the metaphors we've discussed. But as the project developed and the multiple forms of invisible and intangible power emerged as complex and intertwined, it began to feel like a much greater and more radical intervention was also required. Drawing on the values and approaches developed during the last decade in Rialto, including the type of relational power that can be co-produced through collaboration, I now feel compelled to consider how best I can occupy the space of imagining that exists when the script is ripped. As with all the work discussed here, this is an open-ended process that will be shaped by many diverse individuals and forms of knowledge, including those who have been centrally involved in the previous projects, those who have supported them as individuals or in an organis-ational capacity, as well as a range of academics who have engaged with the practice from afar. As is often the case with this work, at this point it is not clear what will emerge, but I believe in the process and the strength of relationships at the core of it, and so time will tell what exactly will unfold next. But I would like to take my lead from three words uttered towards the end of *Natural History of Hope* as one woman speaks out against the voices that argue for staying in line with dominant thinking:

> *Someone has gone to a lot of trouble to write this for us. We need to stick to the script ...*
>
> *... Fuck the script.*

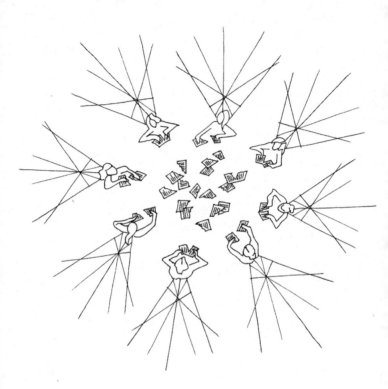

Natural History of Hope

The following are extracts from *Natural History of Hope* (Fiona Whelan, Rialto Youth Project and Brokentalkers, Project Arts Centre, 2016).

Hope is a happy child. She is always smiling. She doesn't see the world as it really is.

She doesn't see the danger or the cruelty. Not yet.

She hasn't learned that there is such a thing as body bags, and there is such a thing as balaclavas.

She hasn't yet experienced the sound a can of cider makes, as it rolls down the stairs of a double-decker bus, followed by one of her parents.

She has never smelled burned hair or charred skin. She has never seen someone getting battered.

She knows nothing about self-harm or sexual violence or a friend's Da that still says hello when he knows well what he did.

She hasn't had to test how loud she can scream. Or heard the sound of her mother screaming.

She hasn't learnt how long a night is when you sit in the corner of a bedroom waiting for the sun to come up.
She hasn't had to see how fast she can unbuckle a seat-belt when under the weight of a local businessman who is making it hard for her to breathe.
She's only a kid. She hasn't learnt how to make her bed or realised that once you make your bed, you're supposed to lie in it.
She doesn't know yet what it takes to raise someone else's kids.
She doesn't know that someday other people will want to talk about her biological clock.
She doesn't know about strangulation or bad drinking.
Or bad panic attacks.
Bad people, bad days.
Bad tempers, bad relationships.
Bad feelings, bad arguments.
Bad seizures, bad neighbours.
Bad advice.

—

Hope is a happy child, she is always smiling,
Her favourite thing in the world is a pair of Cinderella shoes.
She wears them all the time.
They have flat heels and they light up when she walks.
The shoes are covered in glitter.
They have a satin bow and a heart-shaped gemstone on the toe.

Hope feels like a princess in her Cinderella shoes.
Then something happens, something changes.
She notices that all the children in school are wearing
runners, expensive ones, new, clean; not old and worn
out like her Cinderella shoes.
The other children slag her. They point at her
Cinderella shoes and say 'the state of them'. She hates
her Cinderella shoes now. She throws them in the bin
and pretends they are lost so she can get new runners,
just like all the other children.

Hope is in the playground.
She's beating the boys at arm wrestling.
She's smiling. She's happy.
Then something happens, something changes.
She notices that all the girls in the playground are
laughing at her.
She's thinking maybe it's not a good thing to be stronger
than the boys.
She's thinking maybe she has to act more like the
other girls.

—

Can you see it Hope?
The bubble?
We're inside it.
You see everything and everyone through the bubble.
And everyone sees the bubble when they look at you.
They look at you in the bubble. They stare at you.

They make decisions about you. They tell you, you can't. They tell you, you won't. They tell you, you'll never. They measure you with invisible rulers. How good. How bad. How big. How small. How much. How little. You're a number. You're lots of numbers.

They study us.
They observe our behaviour.
They write about us, in books, in newspapers.
They give lectures about us.
When they talk about us, they say words like: working class, underclass, disadvantaged, impoverished, poor, marginalised, oppressed.
They are interested in phenomenology, epistemology, sociology, anthropology.
They say they are doing ethnography, they do case studies, longitudinal studies, empirical research. They even do art projects.
People make their careers trying to understand this bubble, but they will never understand what it's like on the inside.
You will come to love the bubble and hate it.
What does your bubble feel like, Hope?
My bubble feels like a shell on my back. It's heavy.
I hope yours is light and floaty and beautiful. And I hope it's easy to get out of.

———

Hope's son is a real funny boy, a little joker. He loves to mess and dance about.

She fills with joy when she sees the delight in his
little face at birthdays and Christmas and how happy
he is, playing out all day with his friends, only coming
back when he's thirsty.

She treasures her movie nights in bed with him. 'Ma,
can we bring up the popcorn?' he asks, and they gather
up loads of pillows and the two of them lie in her bed,
and he feeds her popcorn while they stare at the telly.
In the morning he helps arrange the cushions and
shake out the duvet and she say, 'You're very good,
you're a great little helper', and he goes all gushy, like
he's the business.

Hope wishes she could erase the memories of all the
bad stuff her son has seen.

She cries when she thinks of his little face going pure
white with fear after running and jumping walls to get
away from danger, the adrenaline pumping in his tiny
body.

She wishes she could change the way his Da is with
him. She wishes his Da would bring him to the park or
the seaside rather than just bringing him to the pub to
watch a United match.

She sees how he loves the outdoors and nature, and
wishes she could bring him on more holidays.

She teaches him the value of money and hard work.
She makes him add up all the prices of the toys he
wants in the Smyth's catalogue and think about how
much his Ma would have to work to earn that money.
On the way to school he sees someone in a BMW and
he asks, 'Ma, how do people get cars?' and she explains

to him that when he is older he will have a good job,
and he will save up and buy his own car.

He asks her, 'Ma, why don't you have a boyfriend?'.

'I just haven't got one son,' she says.

As he gets older, Hope's son will hear his friends talk
about vodka and Red Bull and pints of Bud.

He'll see his older cousin's music videos and say, 'Look
at the tits on her.'

Hope worries about her boy.

She hopes that he'll have the confidence to walk away if
he is ever offered a line of coke or a drag of a joint.

She hopes he treats women with respect.

And that he doesn't see young ones as pieces of meat.

Hope tells him that whether he's into girls or boys, it
doesn't matter.

'I'll love you no matter what,' she says.

She hopes he doesn't get cancer because it runs in the
family.

She hopes he's able to come and talk to her if he's ever
worried about anything.

She hopes he finishes school.

She hopes he finds the career he wants.

She hopes he doesn't grow up to be like his Da.

She hopes he learns how to express his anger without
violence.

And that he is able to step out of the bubble, and see
the world beyond.

She hopes he gets to do all the things she didn't.

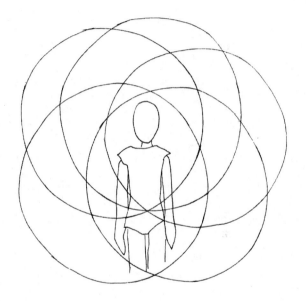

Notes and References

1. Horslips, 1977. 'Sure the Boy Was Green'. From the album *Aliens*. Produced by Alan O'Duffy and Horslips (Dublin: Horslips Records).

2. J.L. Austin, *How to Do Things With Words* (Oxford: Clarendon Press, 1962).

3. W.B. Gallie, 'Essentially Contested Concepts', *Proceedings of the Aristotelian Society*, 56, 1956, pp. 167–98.

4. J.S. Mill, 'On Liberty', in *John Stuart Mill: On Liberty and Other Essays* (Oxford: Oxford University Press, 2004); I. Berlin, *Four Essays on Liberty* (London & New York: Oxford University Press, 1969).

5. See for example P. Pettit, *A Theory of Freedom: From the Psychology to the Politics of Agency* (Cambridge, UK: Polity, 2001).

6. See for example Government of Ireland, *Innovation 2020: Excellence, Talent, Impact: Ireland's Strategy for Research and Development, Science and Technology* (Dublin: Interdepartmental Committee on Science, Technology and Innovation, 2015); Government of Ireland, *Ireland's Competitiveness Challenge 2016* (Dublin: National Competitiveness Council, 2016).

7. M. Foucault, *The Birth of Biopolitics Lectures at the Collège de France, 1978–1979* (Basingstoke: Palgrave Macmillan, 2008); P. Dardot and C. Laval, *The New Way of the World: On Neoliberal Society* (London: Verso, 2013).

8. An example is the Slovenian philosopher Slavoj Žižek. His YouTube channel has over 35,000 subscribers and has recorded almost three million hits since 2013.

9. See for example the European Creative Industries Alliance, http://eciaplatform.eu/about-ecia/ (accessed 16 December 2016).

10. Punctuated by a general strike, with students and workers occupying universities and factories, and also by street battles between protestors and police, the events of May 1968 have been lauded as a revolutionary turning point by some, and lampooned by others as the revolution that never happened.

11. For an overview see M. Haugaard, *Power: A Reader* (Manchester: Manchester University Press, 2002); M. Haugaard and K. Ryan (eds), *Political Power: The Development of the Field* (Opladen, Germany: IPSA and Barbara Budrich, 2012).

12. We have borrowed this terminology from *Powercube*, an online resource developed by the Participation, Power and Social Change team at the Institute of Development Studies, University of Sussex, UK. The project is led by John Gaventa and Jethro Pettit, with communications support by Laura Cornish, https://www.powercube.net/.

13. The idea of intangible power is adapted from Geoffrey Brennan and Phillip Pettit's work on the 'intangible hand' of norm-regulated behaviour. See G. Brennan and P. Pettit, *The Economy of Esteem: An Essay on Civil and Political Society* (Oxford: Oxford University Press, 2004).

14. M. Foucault, 'What is Enlightenment?', in P. Rabinow (ed), *Essential Works of Foucault, 1954–1984, Volume 1: Ethics, Subjectivity and Truth* (New York: The New Press, 1997), pp. 303–20.

15. See DES, *OECD Project Overcoming School Failure: Policies that Work*. National Report Ireland (Dublin: Department of Education and Skills, 2011).

16. I. Hunter, *Re-thinking the School* (St Leonard's, NSW: Allen and Unwin, 1994); W.A.C. Stewart and W.P. McCann, *The Educational Innovators, 1750–1880* (London: Macmillan, 1967); K. Ryan, 'On Power, Habitus, and (In)Civility: Foucault Meets Elias Meets Bauman in the Playground', *Journal of Power*, vol. 1 (3), 2008, pp. 251–74.

17. H. Cunningham, *The Children of the Poor: Representations of Childhood Since the Seventeenth Century* (Oxford: Blackwell, 1992); H. Hendrick, 'Constructions and Reconstructions of British Childhood: An Interpretative Survey, 1800 to the Present', in A. James and A. Prout (eds), *Constructing and Reconstructing Childhood*. 2nd edition (London: Falmer Press, 1997), pp. 33–60; A.M. Platt, *The Child Savers*. 2nd edition (Chicago and London: University of Chicago Press, 1977).

18. M.E. Daly, *The Spirit of Earnest Inquiry: The Statistical and Social Inquiry Society of Ireland, 1847–1997* (Dublin: Statistical and Social Inquiry Society of Ireland, 1997); P. Joyce, *The Rule of Freedom* (London: Verso, 2003).

19. W.N. Hancock, 'The Feasibility of Compulsory Education in Ireland', *Journal of the Statistical Society of London*, vol. 42 (2), 1879, pp. 456–79.

20. M. Carpenter, *Reformatory Schools for the Children of the Perishing and Dangerous Classes* (London: G. Gilpin, 1851).

21. M. Carpenter, *Juvenile Delinquents: Their Condition and Treatment* (London: W. & F.G. Cash, 1853).

22. J. Barnes, *Irish Industrial Schools, 1868–1908: Origins and Development* (Dublin: Irish Academic Press, 1989).

23. N. Rose, *Governing the Soul: The Shaping of the Private Self* (London and New York: Routledge, 1990).

24. See M. Foucault, *Discipline and Punish*, trans. A. Sheridan (London: Penguin, 1977); Hunter, *Re-thinking the School*.

25. An example: Article 28 of the United Nations Convention on the Rights of the Child (ratified by the Irish State in 1992) covers

'the right of the child to education ... with a view to achieving this right progressively and on the basis of equal opportunity', https://www.unicef.org/crc/.

26. See DES, *OECD Project Overcoming School Failure.*

27. Government of Ireland, *A Programme for a Partnership Government* (Dublin: 2016), http://www.merrionstreet.ie/MerrionStreet/en/ImageLibrary/Programme_for_Partnership_Government.pdf.

28. There isn't space to accommodate detailed discussion on the tremendous work accomplished by many teachers and schools, often without adequate state support, and we wish to stress that these critical remarks are aimed at the overarching educational apparatus as shaped and steered by state policy, and in particular the effects of a highly competitive examination system which applies in particular to second- and third-level education in Ireland.

29. Critical analyses of these issues can be found in Z. Bauman, *Work, Consumerism and the New Poor* (Buckingham, Philadelphia: Open University Press, 1998); L. Wacquant, *Punishing the Poor: The Neoliberal Government of Social Insecurity* (Durham and London: Duke University Press, 2009); M. Lazarrato, *Governing by Debt*, trans. J.D. Jordan (South Pasadena, CA: Semiotext(e), 2015).

30. Rush Essay: Professional Academic Writing, http://www.rushanessay.com/.

31. E. Dante and J. Barkat, 'The Shadow Scholar: The Man who Writes Your Student's Papers Tells His Story', *Chronicle Review of Higher Education*, 12 November 2010, http://www.chronicle.com/.

32. A. Sundararajan, 'The "Gig" Economy is Coming. What Will it Mean for Work?', *Guardian Online*, 26 July 2015, https://www.theguardian.com/commentisfree/2015/jul/26/will-we-get-by-gig-economy; W. Hutton, 'The Gig Economy is Here to Stay. So Making it Fairer Must be a Priority', *Guardian Online*, 4 September

2016, https://www.theguardian.com/commentisfree/2016/sep/03/gig-economy-zero-hours-contracts-ethics; S. O'Connor, 'The Gig Economy is Neither "Sharing" nor "Collaborative"', *Financial Times*, 14 June 2016, https://www.ft.com/content/8273edfe-2c9f-11e6-a18d-a96ab29e3c95.

33. As we discuss the field of art in Sections 2 and 3, it is worth noting here that many freelancing artists find themselves in this type of precarious and indebted financial situation. A 2008–09 report on *The Social, Economic & Fiscal Status of the Visual Artist in Ireland,* compiled by Visual Artists Ireland, found that 67 per cent of visual artists in Ireland earn less than €10,000 per annum from their creative work, while 24 per cent earn between €10,000 and €25,000 per annum. Furthermore, 72 per cent do not have a personal pension plan, and are thus likely to experience financial hardship when they retire due to reliance on the state pension. Yet the majority of visual artists who responded to this survey (83 per cent) indicated that they would choose the life of an artist again if given the chance to start over; http://visualartists.ie/advocacy-advice-membership-services/advocacy/advocacy-datasheet-1-topic-the-status-of-the-artist-in-ireland/the-social/. This is important when considering the challenge posed by Yates McKee, who identifies artists as the most privileged among precarious workers and examines how politically engaged artists work in solidarity with other precarious labourers in struggling for social justice. See Y. McKee, *Strike Art: Contemporary Art and the Post-Occupy Condition* (London: Verso, 2016).

34. See P. Leonard, S. Halford and K. Bruce, '"The New Degree?" Constructing Internships in the Third Sector', *Sociology*, vol. 50 (2), 2016, pp. 383–99.

35. The closure of the JobBridge Scheme was announced on 18 October 2016. See Department of Social Protection, http://www.welfare.ie/en/pages/jobbridge-index.aspx.

36. M. O'Halloran, 'Burton Awaits Report on JobBridge Cleaning Posts', *Irish Times*, 20 September 2014, http://www.irishtimes.

com/news/ireland/irish-news/burton-awaits-report-on-jobbridge-cleaning-posts-1.1936498; F. Gartland, 'Backgrounder: JobBridge Controversial from the Start', *Irish Times*, 18 October 2016, http://www.irishtimes.com/news/ireland/irish-news/backgrounder-jobbridge-controversial-from-the-start-1.2834694.

37. Foucault, *The Birth of Biopolitics*; Dardot and Laval, *The New Way of the World*.

38. J. Williams, *Academic Freedom in an Age of Conformity* (Basingstoke: Palgrave Macmillan, 2016), p. 5.

39. All quoted from Williams, *Academic Freedom*, pp. 5, 39–40.

40. Ibid, pp. 5–6, 10.

41. Though we don't discuss this here, the issue of 'post-truth politics' has a bearing on this point. See A. Flood, '"Post-truth" Named Word of the Year by Oxford Dictionaries', *Guardian*, 15 November 2016, https://www.theguardian.com/books/2016/nov/15/post-truth-named-word-of-the-year-by-oxford-dictionaries.

42. On this issue see H.A. Giroux and S.M. Dawes, 'Interview with Henry A. Giroux: The Neoliberalisation of Higher Education', *Simon Dawes: Media Theory, History and Regulation Blog*, https://smdawes.wordpress.com/2014/06/26/interview-with-henry-a-giroux-the-neoliberal isation-of-higher-education/ (accessed 17 November 2015); H.A. Giroux and S.S. Giroux, 'Challenging Neo-liberalism's New World Order: The Promise of Critical Pedagogy', *Cultural Studies, Critical Methodologies*, vol. 6 (2006), pp. 21–32.

43. K. Lynch, B. Grummel and D. Devine, *New Managerialism in Education* (Basingstoke and New York: Palgrave Macmillan, 2012).

44. M. Power, *The Audit Society* (Oxford and New York: Oxford University Press, 1997); M. O'Hara, 'University Lecturers on the Breadline: Is the UK Following in America's Footsteps?', *Guardian*, 17 November 2015, http://gu.com/p/4e6kg/sbl.

45. Presently there are forty-seven countries participating in the Bologna Process, which commenced with the Sorbonne Joint Declaration in 1998, followed by the Bologna Declaration 1999. *European Higher Education Area and Bologna Process*, http://www.ehea.info/article-details.aspx?ArticleId=3 (accessed 2 November 2015).

46. European Association for Quality Assurance in Higher Education, http://www.enqa.eu (accessed 2 November 2015).

47. Dardot and Laval, *The New Way of the World*, pp. 215–54; P. Lipman, 'The Politics of Education Accountability in a Post-9/11 World', *Cultural Studies, Critical Methodologies*, vol. 6 (2006), pp. 52–72; I. MacLaren, 'The Contradictions of Policy and Practice: Creativity in Higher Education', *London Review of Education*, 10 (2012), pp. 159–72; C. Shore and S. Wright, 'Coercive Accountability: The Rise of Audit Culture in Higher Education', in M. Strathern (ed), *Audit Cultures* (London: Routledge, 2000), pp. 57–89; M. Strathern, 'The Tyranny of Transparency', *British Educational Research Journal*, vol. 26 (2000), pp. 309–21; P.T. Webb, 'The Anatomy of Accountability', *Journal of Education Policy*, vol. 20 (2005), pp. 189–208.

48. S. Ingle, 'Russian State Doped More than 1000 Athletes and Corrupted London 2012', *Guardian Online*, 9 December 2016, https://www.theguardian.com/sport/2016/dec/09/more-than-1000-russian-athletes-benefitted-from-state-sponsored-doping.

49. B. Houlihan, *Dying to Win: Doping in Sport and the Development of Anti-doping Policy* (Strasbourg: Council of Europe, 1999); I. Waddington and A. Smith, *An Introduction to Drugs in Sport: Addicted to Winning?* (London and New York: Routledge, 2009.

50. D. Benson, 'Lance Armstrong Exclusive Interview Parts 1–3', *Cyclingnews.com*, 5–10 November 2013, http://www.cyclingnews.com/features/lance-armstrong-exclusive-interview-part-1); T. Hamilton and D. Coyle, *The Secret Race* (London: Bantam Press, 2012.

51. S. Farrand, 'UCI Defend the Creation of an Index of Suspicion', *Cyclingnews.com*, 13 May 2011, http://www cyclingnews.com/news/uci-defend-the-creation-of-an-index-of-suspicion/.

52. WADA, *World Anti-doping Code* (Montreal: World Anti-Doping Agency, 2015), https://www.wada-ama.org/en/resources/the-code/world-anti-doping-code.

53. B. Houlihan, 'Civil Rights, Doping Control, and the World Anti-doping Code', *Sport in Society: Cultures, Commerce, Media, Politics*, vol. 7 (3), 2004, pp. 420–37; A.J. Schneider, 'Privacy, Confidentiality, and Human Rights in Sport', *Sport in Society: Cultures, Commerce, Media, Politics*, vol. 7 (3), 2004, pp. 438–56.

54. B. Sluggett, 'Sport's Doping Game: Surveillance in the Biotech Age', *Sociology of Sport Journal*, vol. 28 (2011), pp. 387–403.

55. S. Farrand, 'Team Sky Releases Froome's Power Data', *Cyclingnews.com*, 18 July 2013, http://www.cyclingnews.com/news/team-sky-releasesfroomes-power-data.

56. *Cycling News*, 'Froome Begins Physiological Testing ahead of Vuelta a España', 17 August 2015, http://www.cyclingnews.com/news/froome-begins-physiological-testing-ahead-of-vuelta-a-espaa/; R. Moore, 'The Hardest Road', *Esquire Magazine*, 7 December 2015, http://chrisfroome.esquire.co.uk/.

57. Hamilton and Coyle, *The Secret Race*; P. Kimmage, *Rough Ride* (London: Yellow Jersey Press/Random House, 2007).

58. *Mouvement Pour un Cyclisme Crédible*, http://www.mpcc.fr/index.php/en/.

59. S.J. Ball, 'The Teacher's Soul and the Terrors of Performativity', *Journal of Education Policy*, vol. 18 (2003), p. 220.

60. See D. Osbourne and T. Gaebler, *Reinventing Government* (Reading, MA: Addison-Wesley, 1992).

61. J. Hoberman, *Testosterone Dreams* (Berkeley: University of California Press, 2005), p. 17.

62. T. Tysome, 'Pills Provide Brain Boost for Academics', *Times Higher Education*, 29 June 2007, https://www.times highereducation.com/news/pills-provide-brain-boost-for-academics/209480.article.

63. Z. Shabbir, 'The Race to the Top: The Use of "Smart Drugs" to Excel in Academia and in the Professional World', *Neuroscience News*, 30 May 2014, http://neurosciencenews.com/the-race-to-the-top-the-use-of-smart-drugs-to-excel-in-academia-and-in-the-professional-world-1060/; M. Quigley, 'Enhancing Me, Enhancing You: Academic Enhancement as a Moral Duty', *Expositions*, vol. 2 (2008), pp. 157–62.

64. ResearchGate, 'RG Score: A New Way to Measure Scientific Reputation', https://www.researchgate.net/publicprofile.RGScore FAQ.html (accessed 12 September 2015).

65. See for example Altmetric.com, which markets its product to publishers, institutions, and researchers, http://www.altmetric. com/ (accessed 16 September 2015).

66. Google Scholar Metrics, https://scholar.google.com/intl/en/ scholar/metrics.html.

67. H. Shema, 'Interview with Richard Price, Academia.edu CEO', *Scientific American*, 31 October 2015, http://blogs. scientificamerican.com/information-culture-interview-with-richard-price-academia-edu-ceo/ (accessed 7 November 2015).

68. Ibid.

69. Ibid.

70. E. Delgado López-Cózar, N. Robinson-García and D. Torres Salinas, 'Manipulating Google Scholar Citations and Google Scholar Metrics: Simple, Easy and Tempting', EC3 Working Papers 6 (2012), http://arxiv.org/ftp/arxiv/ papers/1212/1212.0638.pdf (accessed 13 February 2016).

71. See G. Hall, 'Should This be the Last Thing You Read on Academia.edu?', *Academia.edu* (https://www.academia. edu/16959788/Should_ This_Be_the_Last_Thing_You_Read_ on_Academia.edu (accessed 7 November 2015).

72. Shema, 'Interview with Richard Price'.

73. See D. Trottier, 'Open Source Intelligence, Social Media and Law Enforcement: Visions, Constraints and Critiques', *European Journal of Cultural Studies*, vol. 18 (2015), pp. 530–47.

74. Hall, 'Should This be the Last Thing You Read on Academia. edu?'.

75. M. Foucault, 'The Eye of Power', in C. Gordon (ed), *Power/ Knowledge: Selected Interviews & Other Writings, 1972–1977* (New York: Pantheon, 1980), pp. 146–65.

76. Top-tier professional Taylor Phinney recently expressed such a view in an interview, noting that 'so many kids get burned out in this sport because you throw them into this pressure cooker of numbers that completely takes people away from the sense of actually riding a bike', and he continues by describing what, for him, is 'the essence of the sport': 'exploration, adventure, betterment of mind and body': 'Taylor Phinney: Cycling Needs Saving', *Cycling News*, 16 December 2016, http://www. cyclingnews.com/features/taylor-phinney-cycling-needs-saving/.

77. The painting can be viewed on the website of the *Museo Nacional Centro de Arte Reina Sofia*, http://www.museoreinasofia. es/en/collection/artwork/guernica; a collection of Picasso's sketches are available on Pinterest, https://www.pinterest.com/ mrehunter/images-of-picassos-sketches-for-guernica/. Wikipedia provides images of the German and Soviet Pavilions on its page for the 1937 EXPO, https://en.wikipedia.org/wiki/Exposition_ Internationale_des_Arts_et_Techniques_dans_la_Vie_Moderne.

78. H. Arendt, *The Human Condition*. 2nd edition (Chicago and London: University of Chicago Press, 1958).

79. See M. Foucault, *The Birth of Biopolitics, Lectures at the Collège de France, 1978–1979* (Basingstoke: Palgrave Macmillan, 2008).

80. The multiple genealogies of what is currently referred to as socially engaged art are documented in a number of recent publications, including C. Bishop, *Artificial Hells: Participatory Art and the Politics of Spectatorship* (London and New York:

Verso, 2012); G. Kester, *The One and the Many: Contemporary Collaborative Art in a Global Context* (London: Duke University Press, 2011); G. Sholette, *Dark Matter: Art and Politics in the Age of Enterprise Culture* (New York: Pluto, 2011); N. Thompson (ed.), *Living as Form: Socially Engaged Art from 1991–2011* (New York: Creative Time, 2012).

81. My relationship with Rialto Youth Project developed during a residency in Studio 468, which is based in St Andrew's Community Centre in Rialto. See www://commonground.ie/studio-468/. Studio 468 is a purpose-built community-based art studio in Rialto established in 2003. When it was established it was co-managed by a studio team made up of representatives from the Rialto Development Association, Common Ground, a local arts-development agency and the Dublin City Council Arts Office. I had my first residency there in 2004.

82. J. Koh, *Art-led Participative Processes: Dialogue and Subjectivity Within Performances in the Everyday* (Helsinki: Academy of Fine Arts: University of the Arts, 2015), p. 29.

83. What's the Story? Collective were: Jamie Hendrick, Jonathan Myers, Nichola Mooney, Michael Byrne, Nicola Whelan, Gillian O'Connor, Graham Dunphy, Vanessa Kenny, Garrett Kenny and Fiona Whelan.

84. The new local garda training was co-developed over six weeks during *Policing Dialogues* (September to October 2010) at The LAB by representatives of What's the Story? Collective and Rialto Youth Project in collaboration with An Garda Síochána, and was announced publicly in 2011. Due to the recruitment freeze for Gardaí which saw a temporary closure of the Garda Training College (2011–15) and a series of budget cuts effecting the continuous professional development of existing gardaí, the training could not be implemented. In 2016 discussion regarding the implementation of this local training recommenced.

85. *Natural History of Hope* core group were Rialto Youth Project staff Gillian O'Connor, Dannielle McKenna, Sharon Cooney, Nichola Mooney, Michelle Dunne and artist Fiona Whelan.

86. During my twelve years with Rialto Youth Project, we engaged in four collaborative residencies in Studio 468, in 2004, 2006, 2016 and 2017, the latter two as part of the *Natural History of Hope* project. The 2016 residency was framed as a school with open-ended possibilities, with the period during 2017 focusing specifically on the development of a public performance.

87. *Natural History of Hope* was a live performance by Fiona Whelan, Rialto Youth Project and Brokentalkers, Project Arts Centre, 12–14 May 2016. The primary cast were Audrey Wade, Lydia Lynam, Niamh Tracey, Michelle Dunne, Vicky White, Sharon Cooney, Lisa Graham, Nichola Mooney, Dannielle McKenna, Amy White, Gillian O Connor and Fiona Whelan. The programme and full cast list for the performance is available at www.fionawhelan.com.

88. Professor Kathleen Lynch from UCD School of Social Justice and Dr Martina Carroll (psychologist) acted as advisors to the project, bringing external analyses to the stories and identifying themes related to their respective disciplines, which included these seven social categories identified by Kathleen.

89. The phrase 'the liability of men' emerged from Professor Kathleen Lynch's analysis of the gathered anonymous stories, which included accounts of male violence and male sexual violence over which women felt they lacked control.

90. The historical significance of the Easter Rising of 1916 is anything but straightforward, as can be seen from this brief description from the *Irish Times* website: 'The 1916 Rising was the first major revolt against British rule in Ireland since the United Irishman Rebellion of 1798. Though some see it as an unmandated, bloody act by unrepresentative secret conspirators, for many it was the founding act of a democratic Irish state'; Remembering the 1916 Rising, http://www.irishtimes.com/1916.

91. Waking the Feminists was a grassroots campaign calling for equality for women across the Irish theatre sector that ran from November 2015 to November 2016; www.wakingthefeminists.org.

92. See S. Keating, 'When Feminism Met Real Working-Class Lives in Rialto', *Irish Times*, 28 June 2016, http://www.irishtimes.com/culture/stage/when-feminism-met-real-working-class-lives-in-rialto-1.2696306.

93. A.S. Chassany, 'Marine Le Pen's Hopes of French Presidency Bolstered by Trump', *Financial Times*, 10 November 2016, https://www.ft.com/content/0d03a042-a688-11e6-8b69-02899e8bd9d1.

94. D. McGonagle, '"A New Deal": Museums and Communities – Re-imagining Relations', *Community Development Journal*, vol. 42 (2007), pp. 425–34.

95. I completed the HDip Community Arts Education, NCAD Dublin, 2001–02; MA Art in Public, Ulster University Belfast, 2008–09.

96. F. Whelan and K. Ryan, 'Beating the Bounds of Socially-engaged Art? A Transdisciplinary Dialogue on a Collaborative Art Project with Youth in Dublin, Ireland', *FIELD: A Journal of Socially Engaged Art Criticism*, vol. 4, (spring 2016), http://field-journal.com.

97. Rialto Youth Project (rialtoyouthproject.net).

98. Whelan and Ryan, 'Beating the Bounds of Socially-engaged Art?'.

99. Young person (anonymous), 2008, see F. Whelan, *TEN: Territory, Encounter & Negotiation* (Dublin: Fiona Whelan, 2014), p. 76.

100. C. Mouffe, *Agonistics: Thinking the World Politically* (London and New York: Verso, 2012); C. Mouffe, *On the Political* (Abingdon and New York: Routledge, 2005).

101. Anonymous is an example of a mode of subversive political action called 'hacktivism', meaning activism staged by hacking online platforms, information systems, etc. Anonymous is not a specifiable group of people, and most certainly not an organisation. It is more in tune with the language of anarchism,

that is, an idea that belongs to no one, and thus belongs to everyone. The slogan used by one chapter of Anonymous is: 'We are legion. We do not forgive. We do not forget. Expect us', http://anonofficial.com/, but see also http://anonhq.com/ and http://www.anonews.co/.

102. Whelan and Ryan, 'Beating the Bounds of Socially-engaged Art?'.

103. M. Jackson, *The Politics of Storytelling: Violence, Transgression, and Intersubjectivity* (Copenhagen: University of Copenhagen/ Museum Tusculanum Press, 2002).

104. Arendt, *The Human Condition*.

105. M. Maeckelbergh, 'Doing is Believing: Prefiguration as Strategic Practice in the Alterglobalization Movement', *Social Movement Studies*, vol. 10 (1), 2011, pp. 1–20; S. Springer, 'Fuck Neoliberalism', *ACME: An International Journal for Critical Geographies*, vol. 15 (2), 2016, pp. 285–92.

Bibliography

Arendt, H., *The Human Condition*. 2nd edition (Chicago and London: University of Chicago Press, 1958).

Austin, J.L., *How to Do Things with Words* (Oxford: Clarendon Press, 1962).

Ball, S.J., 'The Teacher's Soul and the Terrors of Performativity', *Journal of Education Policy*, vol. 18, 2003, pp. 215–28.

Barnes, J., *Irish Industrial Schools, 1868–1908: Origins and Development* (Dublin: Irish Academic Press, 1989).

Bauman, Z., *Work, Consumerism and the New Poor* (Buckingham, Philadelphia: Open University Press; 1998).

Benson, D., 'Lance Armstrong Exclusive Interview Parts 1–3', *Cyclingnews.com*, 5–10 November 2013, http://www.cyclingnews. com/features/lance-armstrong-exclusive-interview-part-1.

Berlin, I., *Four Essays on Liberty* (London and New York: Oxford University Press, 1969).

Bishop, C., *Artificial Hells: Participatory Art and the Politics of Spectatorship* (London and New York: Verso, 2012).

Brennan, G. and P. Pettit, *The Economy of Esteem: An Essay on Civil and Political Society* (Oxford: Oxford University Press, 2004).

Carpenter, M., *Juvenile Delinquents: Their Condition and Treatment* (London: W. & F.G. Cash, 1853).

Carpenter, M., *Reformatory Schools for the Children of the Perishing and Dangerous Classes* (London: G. Gilpin, 1851).

Chassany, A.S., 'Marine Le Pen's Hopes of French Presidency Bolstered by Trump', *Financial Times*, 10 November 2016, https://www.ft.com/content/0d03a042-a688-11e6-8b69-02899e8bd9d1.

Cunningham, H., *The Children of the Poor: Representations of Childhood Since the Seventeenth Century* (Oxford: Blackwell, 1992).

Cycling News, 'Taylor Phinney: Cycling Needs Saving', 16 December 2016, http://www.cyclingnews.com/features/taylor-phinney-cycling- needs-saving/.

Cycling News, 'Froome Begins Physiological Testing Ahead of Vuelta a España', 17 August 2015, http://www.cyclingnews.com/news/froome-begins-physiological-testing-ahead-of-vuelta-a-espaa/.

Daly, M.E., *The Spirit of Earnest Inquiry: The Statistical and Social Inquiry Society of Ireland, 1847–1997* (Dublin: Statistical and Social Inquiry Society of Ireland, 1997).

Dante, E. and J. Barkat, 'The Shadow Scholar: The Man who Writes Your Student's Papers Tells His Story', *Chronicle Review of Higher Education*, 12 November 2010, http://www.chronicle.com/.

Dardot, P. and C. Laval, *The New Way of the World: On Neoliberal Society* (London: Verso, 2013).

Delgado López-Cózar, E., N. Robinson-García and D. Torres Salinas, 'Manipulating Google Scholar Citations and Google Scholar Metrics: Simple, Easy and Tempting', EC3 Working Papers 6, 2012, http://arxiv.org/ftp/arxiv/papers/1212/1212.0638.pdf, Accessed 13 February 2016.

DES, *OECD Project Overcoming School Failure: Policies that Work*, National Report Ireland (Dublin: Department of Education and Skills, 2011).

European Association for Quality Assurance in Higher Education, http://www.enqa.eu/ (accessed 2 November 2015.

Farrand, S., 'Team Sky Releases Froome's Power Data', *Cyclingnews.com*, 18 July 2013, http://www.cyclingnews.com/news/team-sky-releasesfroomes-power-data.

Farrand, S., 'UCI Defend the Creation of an Index of Suspicion', *Cyclingnews.com*, 13 May 2011, http://www.cyclingnews.com/news/uci-defend-the-creation-of-an-index-of-suspicion/.

Flood, A., '"Post-truth" Named Word of the Year by Oxford Dictionaries', *Guardian*, 15 November 2016, https://www.theguardian.com/books/2016/nov/15/post-truth-named-word-of-the-year-by-oxford-dictionaries.

Foucault, M., *The Birth of Biopolitics: Lectures at the Collège de France, 1978–1979* (Basingstoke: Palgrave Macmillan, 2008).

Foucault, M., 'What is Enlightenment?', in P. Rabinow (ed.), *Essential Works of Foucault, 1954–1984 Volume 1: Ethics, Subjectivity and Truth* (New York: The New Press, 1997), pp. 303–20.

Foucault, M., 'The Eye of Power', in C. Gordon (ed.), *Power/Knowledge: Selected Interviews & Other Writings, 1972–1977* (New York: Pantheon, 1980), pp. 146–65.

Foucault, M., *Discipline and Punish*, trans. A. Sheridan (London: Penguin, 1977).

Gallie, W.B., 'Essentially Contested Concepts', *Proceedings of the Aristotelian Society*, 56 (1956), pp. 167–98.

Gartland, F., 'Backgrounder: JobBridge Controversial from the Start', *Irish Times*, 18 October 2016, http://www.irishtimes.com/news/ireland/irish-news/backgrounder-jobbridge-controversial-from-the-start-1.2834694.

Giroux, H. A. and S.M. Dawes, 'Interview with Henry A. Giroux: The Neoliberalisation of Higher Education', *Simon Dawes: Media Theory, History and Regulation Blog*, 2014, https://smdawes.wordpress.com/2014/06/26/interview-with-henry-a-giroux-the-neoliberalisation-of-higher-education/, accessed 17 November 2015.

Giroux, H. A. and S.S. Giroux, 'Challenging Neo-Liberalism's New World Order: The Promise of Critical Pedagogy', *Cultural Studies, Critical Methodologies*, vol. 6 (2006), pp. 21–32.

Government of Ireland, *Ireland's Competitiveness Challenge 2016* (Dublin: National Competitiveness Council, 2016).

Government of Ireland, *Innovation 2020: Excellence, Talent, Impact. Ireland's Strategy for Research and Development, Science and Technology* (Dublin: Interdepartmental Committee on Science, Technology and Innovation, 2015).

Government of Ireland, *A Programme for a Partnership Government* (Dublin: 2016), http://www.merrionstreet.ie/MerrionStreet/en/ImageLibrary/Programme_for_Partnership_Government.pdf.

Hall, G., 'Should This be the Last Thing You Read on Academia.edu?', *Academia.edu*, https://www.academia.edu/16959788/Should_This_Be_the_Last_Thing_You_Read_on_Academia.edu, Accessed 7 November 2015.

Hamilton, T. and D. Coyle, *The Secret Race* (London: Bantam Press, 2012).

Hancock, W.N., 'The Feasibility of Compulsory Education in Ireland', *Journal of the Statistical Society of London*, vol. 42 (2), 1879, pp. 456–79.

Haugaard, M., *Power: A Reader* (Manchester: Manchester University Press, 2002).

Haugaard, M. and K. Ryan (eds), *Political Power: The Development of the Field* (Opladen, Germany: IPSA and Barbara Budrich, 2012).

Hendrick, H., 'Constructions and Reconstructions of British Childhood: An Interpretative Survey, 1800 to the Present', in A. James and A. Prout (eds), *Constructing and Reconstructing Childhood*, 2nd edition (London: The Falmer Press, 1997).

Hoberman, J., *Testosterone Dreams* (Berkeley, University of California Press, 2005).

Horslips, 'Sure the Boy Was Green'. From the album *Aliens*. Produced by Alan O'Duffy and Horslips (Dublin: Horslips Records, 1977).

Houlihan, B., 'Civil Rights, Doping Control, and the World Anti-doping Code', *Sport in Society: Cultures, Commerce, Media, Politics*, vol. 7 (3), 2004, pp. 420–37.

Houlihan, B., *Dying to Win: Doping in Sport and the Development of Anti-doping Policy* (Strasbourg: Council of Europe, 1999).

Hunter, I., *Re-thinking the School* (St Leonard's, NSW: Allen and Unwin, 1994).

Hutton, W., 'The Gig Economy is Here to Stay. So Making it Fairer Must be a Priority', *Guardian Online*, 4 September 2016, https://www.theguardian.com/commentisfree/2016/sep/03/gig-economy-zero-hours-contracts-ethics.

Ingle, S., 'Russian State Doped More than 1000 Athletes and Corrupted London 2012', *Guardian Online*, 9 December 2016, https://www.theguardian.com/sport/2016/dec/09/more-than-1000-russian-athletes-benefitted-from-state-sponsored-doping.

Jackson, M., *The Politics of Storytelling: Violence, Transgression, and Intersubjectivity* (Copenhagen: University of Copenhagen/ Museum Tusculanum Press, 2002).

Joyce, P., *The Rule of Freedom* (London: Verso, 2003).

Keating, S., 'When Feminism Met Real Working-Class Lives in Rialto', *Irish Times*, 28 June 2016, http://www.irishtimes.com/ culture/stage/when-feminism-met-real-working-class-lives-in-rialto-1.2696306.

Kester, G., *The One and the Many: Contemporary Collaborative Art in a Global Context* (London: Duke University Press, 2011).

Kimmage, P., *Rough Ride* (London: Yellow Jersey Press/Random House, 2007).

Koh, J., *Art-led Participative Processes, Dialogue and Subjectivity Within Performances in the Everyday* (Helsinki: Helsinki Academy of Fine Arts: University of the Arts Helsinki, 2015).

Lazarrato, M., *Governing by Debt*, trans. J.D. Jordan (South Pasadena, CA: Semiotext(e), 2015).

Leonard, P., S. Halford and K. Bruce, '"The New Degree?" Constructing Internships in the Third Sector', *Sociology*, vol. 50 (2), 2016, pp. 383–99.

Lipman, P., 'The Politics of Education Accountability in a Post-9/11 World, *Cultural Studies, Critical Methodologies*, vol. 6 (2006), pp. 52–72.

Lynch, K., B. Grummel and D. Devine, *New Managerialism in Education* (Basingstoke and New York: Palgrave Macmillan, 2012).

MacLaren, I., 'The Contradictions of Policy and Practice: Creativity in Higher Education', *London Review of Education*, 10 (2012), pp. 159–72.

Maeckelbergh, M., 'Doing is Believing: Prefiguration as Strategic Practice in the Alterglobalization Movement', *Social Movement Studies*, vol. 10 (1), 2011, pp. 1–20.

McGonagle, D., '"A New Deal": Museums and Communities – Re-imagining Relations', *Community Development Journal*, vol. 42 (2007), pp. 425–34.

McKee, Y., *Strike Art: Contemporary Art and the Post-Occupy Condition* (London: Verso, 2016).

Mill, J.S., 'On Liberty', in *John Stuart Mill: On Liberty and Other Essays* (Oxford: Oxford University Press, 2004).

Moore, R., 'The Hardest Road', *Esquire Magazine*, 7 December 2015, Online, http://chrisfroome.esquire.co.uk/.

Mouffe, C., *Agonistics: Thinking the World Politically* (London and New York: Verso, 2012).

Mouffe, C., *On the Political* (Abingdon, UK & New York: Routledge, 2005).

O'Connor, S., 'The Gig Economy is Neither "Sharing" Nor "Collaborative"', *Financial Times*, 14 June 2016, https://www.ft.com/content/8273edfe-2c9f-11e6-a18d-a96ab29e3c95.

O'Halloran, M., 'Burton Awaits Report on JobBridge Cleaning Posts', *Irish Times*, (20 September 2014, http://www.irishtimes.com/news/ireland/irish-news/burton-awaits-report-on-jobbridge-cleaning-posts-1.1936498.

O'Hara, M., 'University Lecturers on the Breadline: Is the UK Following in America's Footsteps?', *Guardian*, 17 November 2015, http://gu.com/p/4e6kg/sbl.

Osbourne, D. and T. Gaebler, *Reinventing Government* (Reading, MA: Addison-Wesley, 1992).

Pettit, P., *A Theory of Freedom: From the Psychology to the Politics of Agency* (Cambridge: Polity, 2001).

Platt, A.M., *The Child Savers*. 2nd edition (Chicago and London: University of Chicago Press, 1977).

Power, M., *The Audit Society* (Oxford and New York: Oxford University Press, 1997).

Powercube, https://www.powercube.net/.

Quigley, M., 'Enhancing Me, Enhancing You: Academic Enhancement as a Moral Duty', *Expositions*, vol. 2 (2008), pp. 157–62.

Rose, N., *Governing the Soul: The Shaping of the Private Self* (London and New York: Routledge, 1990).

Ryan, K., 'On Power, Habitus, and (In)Civility: Foucault Meets Elias Meets Bauman in the Playground', *Journal of Power*, vol. 1 (3), 2008, pp. 251–74.

Schneider, A.J., 'Privacy, Confidentiality, and Human Rights in Sport', *Sport in Society: Cultures, Commerce, Media, Politics*, vol. 7 (3), 2004, pp. 438–56.

Shabbir, Z., 'The Race to the Top: The Use of "Smart Drugs" to Excel in Academia and in the Professional World', *Neuroscience News*, 30 May 2014, http://neurosciencenews.com/the-race-to-the-top-the-use-of-smart-drugs-to-excel-in-academia-and-in-the-professional-world-1060/.

Shema, H., 'Interview with Richard Price, Academia.edu CEO', *Scientific American*, 31 October 2015, http://blogs. scientificamerican.com/information-culture-interview-with-richard-price-academia-edu-ceo/, Accessed 7 November 2015.

Sholette, G., *Dark Matter: Art and Politics in the Age of Enterprise Culture* (New York: Pluto, 2011).

Shore, C. and S. Wright, 'Coercive Accountability: The Rise of Audit Culture in Higher Education', in M. Strathern (ed.), *Audit Cultures* (London: Routledge, 2000).

Sluggett, B., 'Sport's Doping Game: Surveillance in the Biotech Age', *Sociology of Sport Journal*, vol. 28 (2011), pp. 387–403.

Springer, S., 'Fuck Neoliberalism', *ACME: An International Journal for Critical Geographies*, vol. 15 (2), 2016, pp. 285–92.

Stewart, W.A.C. and W. P. McCann, *The Educational Innovators, 1750–1880* (London: Macmillan, 1967).

Strathern, M., 'The Tyranny of Transparency', *British Educational Research Journal*, vol. 26 (2000), pp. 309–21.

Sundararajan, A., 'The "Gig" Economy is Coming. What Will it Mean for Work?', *Guardian Online*, 26 July 2015, https://www. theguardian.com/commentisfree/2015/jul/26/will-we-get-by-gig-economy.

Thompson, N. (ed.), *Living as Form: Socially Engaged Art from 1991–2011* (New York: Creative Time, 2012).

Trottier, D., 'Open Source Intelligence, Social Media and Law Enforcement: Visions, Constraints and Critiques', *European Journal of Cultural Studies*, vol. 18 (2015), pp. 530–47.

Tysome, T., 'Pills Provide Brain Boost for Academics', *Times Higher Education*, 29 June 2007, https://www. timeshighereducation.com/news/pills-provide-brain-boost-for-academics/209480.article.

Wacquant, L., *Punishing the Poor: The Neoliberal Government of Social Insecurity* (Durham and London: Duke University Press, 2009).

WADA, *World anti-doping Code* (Montreal: World Anti-Doping Agency, 2015), https://www.wada-ama.org/en/resources/the-code/world-anti-doping-code.

Waddington, I. and A. Smith, *An Introduction to Drugs in Sport: Addicted to Winning?* (London and New York: Routledge, 2009).

Webb, P.T., 'The Anatomy of Accountability', *Journal of Education Policy*, vol. 20 (2005), pp. 189–208.

Whelan, F., *TEN: Territory, Encounter & Negotiation* (Dublin: Fiona Whelan, 2014).

Whelan, F. and K. Ryan, 'Beating the Bounds of Socially-engaged Art? A Transdisciplinary Dialogue on a Collaborative Art Project with Youth in Dublin, Ireland', *FIELD: A Journal of Socially Engaged Art Criticism*, 4 (spring 2016), http://field-journal.com.

Williams, J., *Academic Freedom in an Age of Conformity* (Basingstoke: Palgrave Macmillan, 2016).

Index

Note: illustrations are indicated by page numbers in bold.